SECOND EDITION

COMMUNICATE CONNECT AND LEAD

A NEW STANDARD FOR INSURANCE ADJUSTERS

DR. KARISSA THOMAS

Efficient Adjuster Publishing

Dedication

To **Arthur Schron Moore, Jr.** A great adjuster and a greater friend. You communicated with calm and clarity, even in chaos. You knew how to make people feel seen—policyholders, peers, everyone. You were deeply knowledgeable, endlessly patient, and always professional. This edition is in honor of the standard you lived by— and the legacy you leave behind.

2024

Acknowledgments

To every insurance adjuster who shows up, file after file, day after day—

Thank you.

This book is for you—the field adjusters walking through homes with collapsed ceilings and heartbroken families. The desk adjusters managing surge volume and late-night calls. The catastrophe adjusters living out of suitcases, writing files between storms. The reviewers, the team leads, the QA specialists, the trainees rising through the ranks.

You are often the invisible bridge between crisis and resolution.

You juggle deadlines, emotions, and expectations with a level of endurance few understand. You absorb frustration without always being thanked. You explain coverage with clarity, even when you're met with blame. You lead conversations with calm when chaos is all around you.

This profession is not easy—but you continue to carry it with grit, compassion, and professionalism.

This edition is my way of honoring you. May it serve as a reminder that your work matters—and that the way you show up, communicate, and lead has impact far beyond the file.

Thank you for raising the standard—one claim, one call, one conversation at a time.

Note from the Author

This second edition was originally published under the title *Communication Skills for Insurance Adjusters: Maximizing Your Value to Insurance Companies While Prioritizing Self-Care.* It has now been expanded, updated, and retitled to better reflect the depth and leadership focus of the content.

Whether you're reading this for the first time or returning to deepen your skills, you'll find that the core message remains the same: communication is not just a technical tool—it's the foundation of trust, clarity, and leadership in every claim.

Contents

How to Use This Book

Communicate, Connect, and Lead: A New Standard for Insurance Adjusters is more than a reference guide—it's a leadership tool. Whether you're an independent adjuster, a desk reviewer, a team lead, or a trainer, this book is structured to support both individual mastery and team development.

Each chapter integrates real-world insight with practical tools, designed to help you improve communication, emotional regulation, and professional presence across every stage of the claims process.

Who This Book Is For

- Independent and staff adjusters navigating high-pressure, emotionally charged environments
- New adjusters building confidence and communication clarity
- Experienced professionals refining their leadership voice
- Team leads and managers coaching others toward excellence

What's Inside

Each chapter includes:

- Real-world scenarios and narratives from the field

- Research-informed strategies for calm, confident communication
- Tools for managing tension, complexity, and human emotion under pressure
- Reflection questions to deepen learning and prompt real-time application

Ways to Use This Book

- **Self-Study**: Use chapter reflections to guide your professional growth
- **Team Meetings**: Assign one chapter per week for group learning and discussion
- **Training Programs**: Integrate into onboarding, CE credit workshops, or internal upskilling
- **Coaching Conversations**: Use stories and strategies as prompts for one-on-one mentorship

For Trainers, Coaches, and Firms

Facilitator guides, team bundles, and licensing options are available for use in structured training environments. If your organization is ready to lead with clarity, care, and credibility—this book can serve as the foundation.

To inquire about bulk orders or access facilitation resources, visit: www.efficientadjuster.net

Preface

A successful insurance adjuster is more than just technically proficient—they are emotionally attuned, communication-savvy, and adaptable under pressure. In today's fast-moving claims environment, soft skills are no longer secondary—they are critical to success. Whether you're negotiating with stakeholders, supporting policyholders during vulnerable moments, or coordinating with colleagues in high-volume operations, your ability to lead with clarity and connect with empathy shapes the outcome and experience of every claim.

This book examines the human aspect of adjusting—what it truly means to communicate, collaborate, and care while navigating an industry founded on precision and policy. Here, we break down the soft skills that define high-performing adjusters: verbal and written communication, active listening, emotional intelligence, empathy, conflict resolution, and professional self-regulation.

Unlike hard skills, which reflect technical knowledge, soft skills are relational. They demonstrate how you interpret tone, manage stress, build trust, and communicate with emotion. These skills shape not just what you say, but also how your words land, how your presence is felt, and how your professionalism is perceived.

For example, effective communication involves more than simply delivering accurate information. It requires adjusting your tone during tense conversations, articulating policy language in plain terms, and listening not just for facts but also for unvoiced feelings. It entails knowing when to pause, when to clarify, and when to establish a firm yet compassionate boundary.

Empathy allows you to connect with policyholders and claimants during moments of loss, frustration, or vulnerability. Active listening ensures that you not only gather facts but also build trust. Emotional intelligence helps you manage your own reactions while reading the room and responding appropriately. Together, these skills enable you to stay composed, respectful, and solution-oriented—even under pressure.

This book also emphasizes one skill that adjusters often overlook: self-care. The demands of the job are real—back-to-back files, emotional labor, compliance pressure, and the constant toggling between field and office realities. To be effective, you must protect your own well-being. This means developing healthy boundaries, learning how to recharge, and practicing emotional discipline—not detachment.

Throughout this book, you'll find practical tools and real-world scenarios tailored to the unique demands of claims work. Whether you're managing property damage, auto losses, injury cases, or catastrophe claims, the principles in these chapters will guide you to lead with integrity and communicate with impact.

Whether you're just starting your journey as an adjuster, aiming to enhance your performance, or seeking a promotion within your company, this book will meet you where you are. It was created to help you strengthen the foundation of your work—your ability to communicate effectively and your capacity to thrive.

Let this be your guide—not only to adjust claims but to adjust confidently, clearly, and compassionately in a complex industry that requires more human leadership.

Author's Note on Stories and Voices

Throughout this book, you will find short first-person stories and reflections woven into various chapters. These narratives are written in a personal voice, yet they are not autobiographical.

Instead, they represent composite field experiences—common moments that adjusters face, drawn from real industry patterns, client insights, and professional reflection. They are designed to capture the emotional and practical challenges of this work in a relatable and resonant way.

Their purpose is simple: to help you see yourself more clearly in your work, without judgment—and to offer a window into the kind of professional presence that can transform pressure into leadership.

Introduction

Insurance adjusting is not just a technical job—it is a profoundly human one. While a strong grasp of policies, procedures, and legal requirements provides the foundation, the true differentiator in this field is your ability to communicate clearly, connect with empathy, and lead with composure and professionalism—even under pressure. This book serves as a guide to the soft skills that make this possible.

Why Communication Matters More Than Ever

Adjusters often serve as the bridge between crisis and resolution. You are the person policyholders turn to when their world has been upended—by damage, loss, injury, or uncertainty. In those moments, your tone, clarity, and presence are just as important as the accuracy of your report or the thoroughness of your file notes.

Whether you are calming an angry claimant, coordinating with team members, or explaining a denial clearly, your communication style shapes not only the outcome of the claim but also the experience—and reputation—surrounding it.

What You'll Learn in These Pages

In the chapters ahead, we will explore the human side of adjusting through seven core domains of professional growth. You will learn to listen actively and ask better questions, strengthen your verbal and written communication skills, deepen your emotional intelligence, and refine your ability to build trust.

You will develop strategies for resolving conflicts and managing challenging moments with composure. You will learn to navigate legal and regulatory obstacles with confidence, and just as importantly, you will receive tools to manage your time, care for your well-being, and sustain your energy for the long haul.

These are not just workplace niceties; they are essential skills that impact your effectiveness, credibility, and resilience. They help you remain grounded under pressure, build rapport with clients, and deliver high-quality service while protecting your mental and emotional bandwidth.

Real Tools for Real Situations

Throughout the book, you will find real-world case studies and practical techniques that can be applied immediately—whether you are conducting a field inspection, managing surge volume, collaborating across departments, or navigating a complex claim with multiple parties.

These are not abstract theories; they are practical strategies specifically designed for adjusters navigating today's fast-paced claims environment.

A Journey of Professional and Personal Growth

This book will enhance your professional communication and encourage personal growth. The most successful adjusters are not only technically proficient; they are self-aware professionals who know how to establish boundaries, manage emotions skillfully, and regain clarity when the chaos of work threatens to overwhelm.

This Book Is for You If...

This book addresses every stage of the adjusting journey. Whether you are new to the field and eager to lead conversations with greater confidence, or a seasoned adjuster looking to enhance your emotional awareness and communication presence, you'll find value here.

If you manage or mentor others, the tools and language on these pages will help you foster a team that communicates with excellence. And if you want to stand out—not just for what you know, but for how you lead, how you listen, and how you respond— then this book is tailored for you.

Communication and Sustainability Go Hand in Hand

While this second edition focuses on skill development, it does not overlook the human cost of this work. Mastery of communication must be combined with sustainability. In every chapter, you will be reminded of the importance of self-care—not as a buzzword, but as a necessary commitment for long-term impact in this high-pressure profession.

You cannot serve effectively if you are depleted. You cannot lead successfully if you are reactive. And you cannot build trust if you are running on empty.

Let's Raise the Standard

Whether you're navigating a claim, coaching a colleague, or correcting misinformation, this book will help you do so with clarity and care. It offers tools, strategies, and language to perform your work not just more efficiently, but more humanely.

Welcome to the updated edition of Communication Skills for Insurance Adjusters.

Let's raise the standard—one conversation at a time.

Part I

Communication Foundations

Before an adjuster can lead with confidence, navigate difficult conversations, or build lasting rapport with clients and colleagues, they must first master the fundamentals of communication. This is not merely a soft skill or an optional bonus—it is the foundation upon which every claim, every interaction, and every outcome is built.

In this section, we explore the foundational building blocks of effective communication in insurance adjusting. These core skills will support you across every facet of your work—from navigating emotionally charged conversations with policyholders to producing accurate, legally sound documentation. They influence how you collaborate with underwriters, estimators, contractors, and carrier representatives. Most importantly, they shape how you are perceived: reactive or responsive, vague or clear, transactional or trustworthy.

We begin by examining the vital role communication plays in shaping trust and credibility. From there, we explore the difference between hearing and truly listening—between gathering facts and understanding context. We consider how tone, body language, and nonverbal signals can affect the emotional direction of an encounter, for better or worse. We also look at the written aspect of the work: how to write clearly and compliantly without losing the human touch. Throughout, we return to a guiding principle—great adjusters ask better questions. Not just to check boxes, but to uncover the full story behind the loss.

Every claim begins with a conversation. Sometimes it's verbal, sometimes it's written, and sometimes it's simply the energy we bring into a space. What matters most is that those first impressions—and every one that follows—are intentional, grounded, and constructive.

Let's start with why communication is so important in this role and what makes it so complex in the world of adjusting.

Chapter 1

The Importance of Communication in Insurance Adjusting

Communication is not a secondary skill in insurance adjusting—it is the essence of the work. Every claim begins and concludes with a conversation, whether it's verbal or written, digital or in person. As an adjuster, your ability to communicate clearly, calmly,

"Your voice travels farther than your ladder. Communication is your most influential tool in this job."

and credibly has a direct impact on how policyholders perceive the claims process—and how insurance companies assess your performance.

In the modern claims environment, technical accuracy alone isn't enough. The most effective adjusters are those who can manage tone during tension, explain coverage clearly, and ask questions that reveal not only what happened, but also how people are feeling. Communication is how you gather information, build trust, reduce friction, and move the claim forward. When done well, it enhances the entire process. When done poorly, it creates confusion, delays, and dissatisfaction.

Whether you are managing property damage, liability, catastrophe claims, or virtual desk work, your day consists of conversations—many of which are emotionally charged. You may speak with a policyholder who has just experienced a devastating loss, a contractor pushing for supplemental approval, or a carrier representative needing documentation. In each case, your communication choices shape the direction and tone of that interaction.

Communication as a Professional Tool

Your ability to explain complex policy language in plain, respectful terms is one of the most powerful assets you bring to this work. Most clients will not remember the exact dollar amount of a depreciation schedule or the fine print of their deductible clause—but they will absolutely remember how they were spoken to. They will recall whether their concerns were acknowledged, if they felt rushed or dismissed, or if your explanation left them more confused than when the conversation began. Respectful, well-paced communication is often the difference between a satisfied client and a complaint.

The same holds true for written communication. File notes, emails, and official documentation are not just administrative tasks; they represent your professional voice on record. Each written entry reflects your judgment, attention to detail, and your ability to represent the company with clarity and precision. A well-written note can protect you legally and enhance your standing with supervisors, while a poorly written one can expose gaps in your process or create unnecessary friction.

When communication is careless, its impact is often subtle at first but becomes significant over time. A vague or rushed email can lead to confusion and necessitate extra follow-up. A defensive tone during a policyholder call can escalate tension. Missed emotional cues during an inspection can create distance, even when the facts are technically correct. Furthermore, failing to explain what happens next—regardless of how minor the step—is likely to leave a claimant feeling ignored or abandoned.

These lapses not only slow down the claims process but also quietly erode trust, leaving clients and colleagues uncertain about your commitment, competence, or care. In a profession founded on credibility and service, this erosion can cost more than just time—it can jeopardize your reputation.

Human-Centered Communication in High-Stress Moments

What makes communication especially complex in adjusting is the emotional weight behind it. Often, you're delivering news people don't want to hear: that their loss isn't covered, that their documentation is incomplete, or that their check will be less than expected. You might also be the first person to speak to them after a crisis.

This is where emotional intelligence becomes indispensable. It is not simply about being polite—it is about being emotionally present and attuned to how your tone, timing, and language influence someone's ability to hear, process, and respond to what you are communicating. Great adjusters do more than "get the claim done." They make the process more human—without losing clarity or authority. They know how to speak with confidence, yet without coldness. They can set firm boundaries without showing defensiveness. They can manage their own stress and tone while guiding others through theirs.

THE FIRST CALL AFTER THE FIRE

I will never forget the call. The file had just been assigned—structure fire, partial loss, policyholder on site. I dialed the number, expecting a straightforward intake. Instead, I encountered a silence so heavy it filled the line.

When she finally spoke, her voice cracked with every other word. She had lost her pets. She had just watched fire-fighters break down her front door and pour water over her memories. I could hear the crunch of debris beneath her feet as she paced outside what was left of her living room. And there I was, asking her to verify her policy number.

I caught myself mid-sentence.

"I'm so sorry," I said. "Before we go any further—I want you to know I hear how hard this is. I'm here to help walk you through it, one step at a time. You're not alone."

The shift was instant. Her breathing slowed. Her answers became steadier. We still had to discuss the deductible, the contents list, and the temporary housing—but now, we were doing it together. That wasn't because I had the right check-list. It was because I remembered to bring my humanity into the conversation.

I didn't solve her crisis. I didn't rebuild her home. But I did offer something else: a voice that didn't make her pain feel like an inconvenience. That's what communication is in this work—a bridge between policy and person. And that's when I began to understand: the most important tool I carry into a claim is not just my software or my scope—it's my presence.

Why Communication Is Your Competitive Advantage

Strong communication skills enhance your value to carriers, firms, and clients in measurable and meaningful ways. When you communicate with clarity and confidence, you can close claims more efficiently, reducing unnecessary delays that frustrate both the policyholder and the carrier. Additionally, you are more likely to de-escalate tense conversations before they escalate into formal complaints, which protects your professional standing and fosters a positive claims experience.

Clear, consistent communication strengthens relationships with clients and colleagues alike. It enables you to represent your firm with professionalism, even in high-pressure situations, and positions you as someone trustworthy with complex files. Over time, these habits foster a reputation for fairness, responsiveness, and sound judgment.

Most importantly, strong communication protects your time. When expectations are clearly set, documentation is thorough, and tone is respectful yet firm, you spend less time revisiting misunderstandings and more time moving claims forward. In an industry where your performance is constantly evaluated through both speed and service, your communication skills are not just helpful—they are your differentiator. They allow you not only to survive in this role but also to stand out.

🔍 End-of-Chapter Reflection

Use the questions below to apply what you've learned, strengthen your awareness, and grow your confidence as a communicator.

1. *When do I feel most clear and confident in my communication—and when do I tend to withdraw, react, or rush?*

2. *What impact does my tone or language have on the people I serve? How can I adjust it to create more clarity and calm?*

3. *What would it look like to treat communication not as a task—but as a tool to lead every interaction well?*

Chapter 2

Listening Skills

In the world of insurance adjusting, listening is more than a courtesy—it is a vital performance skill. It determines how effectively you understand a claim, how well you build trust, and how confidently you navigate tense situations. At its

> *"Listening isn't about waiting to speak—it's about making space for what matters."*

best, listening transforms routine conversations into meaningful exchanges and allows you to represent your firm with the kind of professionalism that clients remember long after the file is closed.

Yet in the fast pace of daily operations, listening often becomes a mere task. Adjusters may focus on completing scripts or gathering surface-level details, nodding along while mentally preparing their next response. This type of reactive hearing can advance a claim, but it seldom leaves clients feeling seen or understood. In this work, that emotional clarity holds equal importance to procedural accuracy.

The Power of Intentional Listening

True listening is not passive; it is active, deliberate, and strategic. It requires you to quiet the mental noise, create space for the full story, and attend not only to the facts but also to the emotional context beneath them. Listening with this depth allows you to catch important details that others may miss. It enables you to sense frustration before it escalates and to respond in a way that validates the client's experience while still advancing the claim forward.

The difference between hearing and listening is simple—but significant. Hearing is automatic; you do not have to try to hear a person's voice. However, to listen—to truly listen—you must focus completely on the speaker. You must be willing to pause your own inner dialogue and give your full attention to the words, tone, and unspoken subtext that often reveal the deeper truth.

Listening attentively helps you understand what happened— not just from a technical perspective, but from the policyholder's lived experience. It enables you to detect emotional shifts and uncover hidden concerns, even when they aren't explicitly voiced. Additionally, it allows you to build rapport more quickly, reduce defensiveness, and foster a sense of safety within even the briefest interactions. It also minimizes the risk of repeating questions or missing critical details—both of which can undermine a claimant's confidence in your process.

Sometimes, the person you are speaking with may feel overwhelmed. Their story might be scattered, and they may speak in circles, driven more by emotion than by sequence. In such moments, listening requires patience and emotional regulation. It asks you to remain grounded, providing just enough reassurance to keep the conversation steady without rushing them past what they need to express.

THE WINDOW THAT WASN'T ABOUT THE WINDOW

It was a hail claim—minor damage, no coverage issues, and a straightforward inspection. I was ready to wrap things up quickly. However, as I stood in the living room, the policyholder pointed to a cracked window and inquired why it wasn't being included. I clarified that the damage didn't seem recent. She nodded but didn't stop there.

She started talking about her husband, who had passed away last winter, and how that window had been his favorite spot. She spoke of how the hailstorm, brief as it was, had shaken her more than she expected. I could tell this wasn't about the estimate anymore—it was about the grief that had been waiting for a witness.

I let her speak. I didn't interrupt to redirect the conversation. I didn't speed it up, even though I had two more inspections that afternoon. I simply stood there and listened. When she finished, she looked at me and said, "Thank you. I just needed someone to hear that."

The window wasn't covered; that remained unchanged. However, her reaction to that news did change. She didn't feel dismissed; instead, she felt heard.

That day reminded me that listening isn't a delay in the claims process; it's part of the work. Giving someone your full attention can take less than five minutes, and in return, you often receive something far more valuable than compliance: cooperation, calm, and respect.

Staying Present Under Pressure

Listening becomes especially difficult when the stakes are high—when claim volume surges, when you're behind on file notes, or when the person on the other end of the line is angry or emotionally overwhelmed. These are moments when you may find yourself slipping into problem-solving mode, crafting a response while the other person is still speaking or rushing to end the call so you can move on to the next one.

But the most effective adjusters learn to resist that impulse. They stay present, even during uncomfortable conversations. They understand that silence is not always inefficiency; it can be the pause that builds trust. They listen not to finish tasks faster, but to do them better. That subtle shift in mindset separates transactional service from professional excellence.

Listening is not merely a passive activity; it requires discipline. In the emotionally complex world of insurance adjusting, it stands out as one of the most powerful disciplines you can cultivate.

🔍 End-of-Chapter Reflection

Use the questions below to evaluate your listening habits and identify small but powerful ways to improve the quality of your presence in every conversation.

1. *When do I tend to listen fully—and when do I find myself preparing to respond instead of truly hearing?*

2. *What signals tell me that someone is not feeling heard, even if I've listened technically?*

3. *How can I create more moments in my workflow to slow down, listen actively, and respond more intentionally?*

Chapter 3

Verbal and Non-Verbal Communication

As an adjuster, the words you speak— and the way you carry yourself— become part of the claim file, the policyholder's memory, and the culture of your team. While verbal communication often takes center stage in claims work, your non-verbal cues convey just as much. Together, they shape how others perceive your presence.

"People don't just hear your words— they feel your posture, your pause, your presence."

When people remember a conversation, they rarely recall your exact wording. What stays with them is how they felt. They remember whether your tone calmed or escalated the moment. They remember whether your body language created space or built distance. They remember if your voice conveyed clarity, confidence, or condescension. This is why verbal and non-verbal communication are inseparable in adjusting. You are never just delivering information—you are shaping perception, expectation, and emotion every time you interact.

How You Say It Matters

Two adjusters can express the same sentence and produce two entirely different outcomes. One adjuster may sound composed, compassionate, and reassuring, while the other may come across as cold, rushed, or disengaged—even if both are technically correct in what they said. In this line of work, accuracy is important, but tone determines whether that accuracy is received.

Policyholders often reach out when facing emotionally difficult situations. A car has been totaled. A roof has collapsed. A home feels unsafe. In those fragile moments, your tone signals whether they are in good hands—or just another file number.

It is not just the speed of your voice or the firmness of your words; it is the breath you take before delivering difficult news. It is your willingness to slow down when someone asks you to repeat something. It is the steadiness you bring when someone begins to panic and the warmth that lingers even when you are setting a boundary. These choices are not about personality—they are about intention.

Tone is not just a soft skill; it is a performance skill that can be measured by how others respond to you in high-pressure situations.

THE ACCUSATION THAT CHANGED MY APPROACH

It occurred on a Thursday morning. I was following up on a denied claim related to a roofing dispute—clear wear and tear, no coverage, and multiple prior inspections. I was prepared, with my file notes, reference dates, and documentation in order. I called the homeowner, anticipating a quick explanation.

She interrupted me almost immediately. "You people never care," she said, her voice sharp. "You talk to us like we're stupid."

I felt my defenses rise. I hadn't said anything disrespectful. I hadn't even gotten through my first sentence. My instinct was to push back, to prove that I was just doing my job. But something in her voice stopped me. It wasn't just anger—it was hurt. She didn't want a better explanation; she wanted to feel respected.

I paused. Then I said, "I can hear how frustrating this has been for you. Let's walk through it together, and I'll do my best to make this part feel more clear."

Her tone softened. We still ended the call with the same coverage outcome. But by the end, she was thanking me for listening and for "talking to her like a person."

That moment changed how I approached every claim thereafter. I realized that professionalism isn't just what you say—it's how you say it, especially when someone expects not to be heard.

What Your Body Says—Even Over the Phone

Non-verbal communication includes your eye contact, facial expressions, posture, gestures, and even how you manage silence. In person, these cues convey powerful messages. An open stance signifies receptiveness. A calm face reflects steadiness. Eye contact indicates engagement. These subtle details often foster trust more effectively than words ever could.

But even in remote settings—whether on the phone or over video—non-verbal energy still comes through. A smile can be heard in your tone. A sigh can reveal frustration. A distracted rhythm in your pacing can signal to the other person that they are not your priority. People—especially those in distress—become highly attuned to how something is being communicated. Even when you are trying to remain neutral, multitasking or emotional fatigue can seep through your voice.

You may believe you're simply being efficient. However, if you sound impatient, clipped, or disinterested, the person on the other end will take notice. They will begin to draw conclusions about your professionalism, care, and credibility—regardless of what your words intended.

Communicating with Intention

Great communicators in this industry do more than just speak clearly. They prepare for challenging conversations. They pause to consider how their words will be received. They know when to explain again and when to simply listen. They adapt their delivery not to placate, but to connect. They understand that every claim is a legal and financial transaction—and also a profoundly human one.

As an adjuster, you are not a customer service representative following a script. You are a licensed professional operating at the intersection of emotion, responsibility, and urgency. That role demands more than just precise wording. It requires grounded, emotionally intelligent communication—especially in moments when it would be easier to shut down or rush through.

This chapter is not only about learning what to say; it is about becoming more aware of how you say it, how you carry it, and how your presence communicates—before and beyond your words.

🔍 End-of-Chapter Reflection

Use these questions to deepen your awareness of how your verbal and non-verbal habits shape the experience of those you serve.

1. **When was the last time someone misunderstood my tone or body language—and what might I have done differently?**

2. **How do I want people to feel after an interaction with me— and what part of my delivery helps or hinders that?**

3. **What small shift in my communication style would make me more grounded, present, or professional?**

Chapter 4

Written Communication

In insurance adjusting, your writing is not just a record—it reflects your thinking, professionalism, and credibility. Long after the phone call ends or the inspection is complete, your written words remain. Whether it's a file note, an email, or a report, what you write becomes part of the permanent claim history and represents how you operate.

"Your goal isn't to write beautifully—it's to write responsibly."

Strong written communication does not require you to sound like a lawyer or write like an author. It means that your writing is clear, accurate, respectful, and aligned with its purpose. It involves saying what needs to be said—no more, no less—and doing so in a way that fosters trust and avoids confusion.

For adjusters, writing must achieve three objectives: document, inform, and protect. You document to create a record of your actions and decisions. You inform to ensure that others—policyholders, supervisors, or legal teams—can comprehend the logic of your process. And you protect both yourself and your company by eliminating ambiguity, bias, and emotion from the record.

Your goal isn't to write beautifully—it's to write responsibly.

The Weight of a Well-Written Note

In many firms, adjusters are evaluated on documentation as much as on resolution. Your notes narrate the story of the claim. They indicate whether you asked the right questions, followed protocol, explained coverage accurately, and closed the file professionally. A vague or incomplete note leaves too much open to interpretation—and that is often where disputes, confusion, or liability begin.

Consider the difference between a simple "Spoke with insured" and a more detailed entry: "Called insured at 3:30 PM. Discussed roof damage and deductible responsibilities. Insured asked about timeline. Explained next steps and inspection expectations. No concerns expressed." The second note does not merely fill space; it demonstrates clarity, intention, and control. If that file is reviewed weeks or months later, the complete context will remain intact.

Great documentation doesn't take longer; it saves time later by preventing unnecessary questions, backtracking, and miscommunication.

THE EMAIL THAT CAUSED A STORM

It was a typical midweek morning when our team lead forwarded an email chain that had escalated quickly. A newer desk adjuster had sent a denial letter to a policyholder, copying the contractor and the carrier. The content itself was accurate, but the tone was flat, technical, and cold. There was no greeting, no context—just a three-sentence explanation that read like a legal dismissal.

By the next morning, the policyholder had called twice, the contractor had filed a complaint, and our manager was questioning why this had escalated into a reputational issue.

We gathered as a team to review the message. The lesson wasn't about the decision—it was about the delivery. The adjuster had not intended to sound dismissive. In fact, she was trying to be efficient. However, in her effort to be brief, she lost control of the tone. The email landed like a closed door.

Together, we rewrote the message. It still conveyed the same outcome, but this time with care: a brief acknowledgment of the situation, a clear explanation of the denial, and an open offer to discuss further if needed. We didn't just clean up one email—we established a new standard for documenting denials in writing.

That day changed our approach to written communication as a team. We realized that clarity is only one part of the equation. The other part is emotional accuracy—writing in a way that conveys authority without sacrificing humanity.

Writing as a Reflection of Your Presence

Tone is just as important in written communication as it is in person. However, many adjusters fall into two predictable traps: being too casual or excessively formal. Casual writing can appear careless or unprofessional, while rigid, overly complex language can seem cold, bureaucratic, or even condescending.

Finding the right tone means writing the way you would speak when you are at your professional best—clear, confident, and grounded. It involves skipping phrases that feel like filler, such as "just checking in" or "hope this helps," and instead choosing to write with intention and ownership. Likewise, you don't need to mimic legal documents to sound credible. A well-structured paragraph, written in natural yet precise language, will build trust far more effectively than a dense wall of legal jargon.

When you write an email, an update, or a note in the file, ask yourself: Will the reader feel more informed or overwhelmed? Am I using language that makes this easier to understand or harder?

Writing to Manage, Not Just Maintain

Adjusters who write effectively do more than document— they manage. They manage expectations, timelines, and tension. Effective writing reduces unnecessary follow-ups and clarifies ambiguity. It drives people toward action and resolution instead of circling back for clarification.

In remote or high-volume environments, where you may never meet the policyholder or your team face-to-face, your writing serves as your voice. It communicates on your behalf long after the task is complete. Whether read by a supervisor, a policyholder, or a legal auditor, it should consistently reflect your professionalism and care.

🔍 End-of-Chapter Reflection

Use these questions to reflect on how your writing shapes outcomes, sets tone, and protects your professional presence.

1. *What does my writing say about how I think and lead? Is it rushed, clear, reactive, confident?*

2. *When was the last time a misunderstanding came from unclear notes or emails—and what can I learn from it?*

3. *How can I make my writing more intentional—especially when under time pressure or emotional stress?*

Chapter 5

Questioning Techniques

The questions you ask shape the answers you receive—and in claims adjusting, those answers can determine everything from coverage decisions to customer satisfaction. However, effective questioning is not just about gathering data. It involves guiding the conversation, building rapport, and creating space for clarity to emerge.

"The best adjusters don't interrogate; they investigate—with empathy."

In emotionally charged or high-stress situations, people rarely respond with complete, linear narratives. They may offer fragments, lead with emotion rather than facts, or become silent and defensive. In those moments, the way you frame a question can either create a pathway forward or shut the conversation down.

The best adjusters don't interrogate; they investigate—with empathy. They ask not only what happened, but also how it felt, what was observed, what has changed, and what support is needed. They understand that questioning is not about control; it's about connection. And when questions are posed with that intention, even the most difficult conversations begin to soften.

"WHAT AM I MISSING?"

It happened during a team review meeting. One of our senior adjusters had just closed a file that seemed clean on the surface: water damage, clear limits, repairs underway, and a satisfied policyholder. However, something in the documentation raised concerns. A supervisor asked why a contractor's supplement had been denied without further inquiry. The adjuster replied with confidence: "It didn't look reasonable, so I closed it."

There was a pause. Then a colleague gently asked, "Did you reach out to the contractor directly before denying it?"

The adjuster hesitated. "No. I assumed they were inflating it."

That moment shifted the room. Not because the denial was necessarily wrong—but because the questioning process had been rushed. There had been an opportunity to ask one more question, make one more call, and potentially gain key insight that could have protected both the file and the relationship.

Later that day, the adjuster approached the colleague and said, "Thanks for asking what you did. I think I've been approaching questions as a task to get through, not a tool to get better. Next time, I'll pause and ask: What am I missing?"

That one question became a mantra across our team—not only for catching errors but also for staying humble, curious, and open.

Framing Questions with Intention

There is an art to asking questions in a way that fosters psychological safety. Open-ended questions tend to invite richer responses, allowing individuals to express themselves more fully.

Asking, "Can you walk me through what happened?" creates a much different tone than "Did the water enter through the ceiling?" The first builds connection and context, while the second seeks a fact—sometimes too soon.

The timing and emotional tone of your questions matter just as much as their wording. If you approach a conversation with stress or urgency, the other person is likely to reflect that energy back. However, if you take a breath, slow down, and ask with calm curiosity, you make it easier for the other party to do the same. Your emotional posture guides theirs.

Whether you're documenting a file, clarifying coverage, or interviewing a contractor on-site, your job is to gather the information that matters—clearly, thoroughly, and respectfully. Often, this means listening deeply between your questions to grasp what needs to be asked next.

Reading the Room and Reading the Moment

Not every question needs to be asked in the first conversation. Sometimes, delaying the best question is essential—because the person in front of you is still processing, grieving, or feeling overwhelmed. In those moments, it may be more effective to build rapport, ground the conversation, or set expectations before moving into investigative details.

Strong adjusters understand how to read the moment. They know when to dig in and when to step back. They rely on awareness rather than solely on scripts. Asking a question too early— even if it's the right one—can create resistance. However, posing it at the right time, in the right tone, and with the right presence builds trust.

Even within your organization, the way you ask questions matters. Asking a teammate, "What am I missing?" invites collaboration instead of critique. Asking your manager, "What would success look like in this situation?" reframes the conversation into a one of clarity rather than frustration. Great adjusters don't just manage claims—they model curiosity as a professional habit.

Creating Space for Better Answers

The best questions aren't always the ones with the quickest answers. They are the ones that create space for reflection, reveal gaps, and uncover perspectives or possibilities that weren't obvious at first. When you lead a conversation with thoughtful questioning, you don't just collect data—you create understanding.

Over time, this kind of intentional questioning becomes second nature. You begin to recognize when someone is withholding details, not out of deceit, but because they haven't yet been given the language or safety to express them. You recognize when a conversation needs structure—and when it needs grace. Moreover, you learn that your voice isn't your only tool; your curiosity is equally powerful.

🔍 End-of-Chapter Reflection

Use these questions to explore how your questioning style affects your clarity, relationships, and professional growth.

1. *When do I feel most confident asking questions—and when do I hold back or rush through them?*

2. *How can I ask more questions that invite clarity instead of control?*

3. *What's one thing I could change this week about how I guide conversations through questioning?*

Chapter 6

Documentation as a Communication Skill

Documentation isn't just a task to check off—it's a core part of how you communicate as an adjuster. It serves as your voice on paper, your professional presence in the claim file, and your protection when memories fade or disputes arise. More than any con-

"Your notes are your legacy. They tell the story long after your voice is gone."

versation or phone call, it is the one aspect of your work that will be read, reviewed, and relied upon long after you've moved on to the next file.

In many ways, your notes reflect your reputation. They detail how you managed the claim, what you observed, how you interacted with the policyholder, and how you made decisions. Additionally, they showcase your thought processes, comprehension of coverage, and the level of clarity—or confusion—you convey to others.

For adjusters, documentation serves multiple purposes: it records the facts, justifies actions, and ensures continuity if the file is reassigned. In complex or contested claims, documentation may be reviewed by legal teams, auditors, or even presented in court. This means it must be professional, precise, and complete— not perfect, but purposeful.

THE FILE THAT SPOKE LOUDER THAN I MEANT

It was a significant loss—multiple rooms affected, a frustrated contractor, and a policyholder who had been waiting for over a month for progress. I had inherited the file midstream, and the first thing I did was pull up the notes. I expected the usual: summaries, inspection logs, and a few phone call recaps. What I found instead made me pause.

"Policyholder is being unreasonable—complains every time I call."

"Contractor doesn't understand the scope—wasting my time."

"Will try to get this closed. Tired of going in circles."

No names. No dates. No explanation of decisions. The notes weren't just vague—they were emotionally charged. As I read, I realized two things: first, I lacked a clear timeline of events. Second, the tone of the documentation had already shaped my expectations of the people involved—and not in a constructive way.

I had to start from scratch by calling the contractor, clarifying with the policyholder, and rebuilding trust all over again. More importantly, it made me stop and ask: what do my notes say about me when I'm not there to speak?

I went back and reviewed a few of my recent files. Some were solid, but others carried traces of my frustration: short phrases, passive-aggressive wording, and incomplete summaries. It was a wake-up call. I realized that my writing didn't just capture what happened; it shaped how others would perceive the people and the process. I wasn't just documenting; I was narrating. And I had a responsibility to do it well.

Writing for the Reader

One of the most common mistakes adjusters make is assuming they're writing only for themselves. In reality, you're writing for your future self, your supervisor, your client, or anyone else who may touch the file. If your notes are too vague, too brief, or emotionally charged, they create confusion—and confusion invites complications.

Every note you write should address several unspoken questions: What happened? What did you observe or discuss? What decision did you make? And why did you make it?

Equally important, is the tone neutral? Is the language respectful? Could someone reading this months later understand what happened and why?

Clarity doesn't require complexity. In fact, the best documentation is often the most straightforward—short sentences, a clean structure, and a clear account of events. Good writing demonstrates your attention, while great writing illustrates that you are leading the claim, not simply reacting to it.

Your Documentation Is Your Shield

Even when you do everything right, some claims may still be challenged. Contractors might dispute your estimates. Policyholders may forget what was communicated. Supervisors may request clarification weeks after a file has been closed. In those situations, your documentation serves as your shield.

A detailed and professional note protects your memory, decisions, and professional integrity. The more precise your wording, the clearer your reasoning. Such clarity fosters trust and often prevents further escalation.

And just as your documentation can protect you, its absence—or tone—can expose you. What you leave out, or how you express it, can unintentionally undermine the strength of your file. That's why every note matters. It may seem routine—but it can become pivotal.

The Emotional Layer of Written Records

It's easy to view documentation as mechanical. However, your writing carries emotional weight, whether intended or not. A sarcastic comment, a dismissive phrase, or a frustrated tone—even if directed at a contractor or internal contact—can influence how others perceive your professionalism.

Notes that express irritation or judgment send subtle signals to your team, supervisors, and yourself. Over time, these notes can reinforce a reactive mindset instead of a thoughtful one.

The standard isn't perfection—it's professionalism. Your notes should reflect the same calm, clear, and emotionally intelligent presence that you aim to bring to live interactions. When someone reads your file, they should feel that the claim was handled by someone in control—someone fair, composed, and clear-headed, regardless of how difficult the situation may have been.

🔍 End-of-Chapter Reflection

Use these questions to refine how your documentation habits support or challenge your professionalism.

1. *When was the last time I reviewed one of my own file notes and felt it didn't reflect my best thinking? What would I revise?*

2. *Do my notes serve the next person who touches the file—or do they assume too much?*

3. *How can I improve the tone and clarity of my documentation without adding unnecessary time or effort?*

Part II

Emotional Intelligence & Human Interaction

Strong communication isn't just about what you say—it's about how you connect. It's the tone you convey when delivering tough news, the patience you maintain in difficult moments, and the emotional awareness you bring to every situation.

This section explores the emotional and relational core of adjusting work. In this industry, your ability to stay calm, read people, manage conflict, and connect under pressure isn't just a soft skill—it's a survival skill.

You will move beyond the mechanics of communication to embrace the emotional intelligence necessary for effectively leading yourself and others. You will explore the role of empathy, learn to manage emotionally charged situations with presence, and develop the interpersonal skills that turn conflict into clarity and tension into trust.

Whether you are dealing with a distressed policyholder, a contentious contractor, or a colleague under pressure, your response is important. These chapters will guide you in cultivating greater steadiness, intentionality, and humanity in your workplace interactions.

Because every claim represents more than just paperwork; it's a moment in someone's life. How you show up in that moment matters.

Chapter 7

Emotional Intelligence

It's easy to assume that adjusting is solely about facts: scope, coverage, liability, documentation. However, behind every fact is a person. Behind every file is a story. And behind every outcome is an emotional experience—for both the policyholder and the adjuster managing the claim.

"Emotional intelligence isn't about staying calm—it's about knowing when you've reached your limit and choosing not to override it."

That's where emotional intelligence comes in.

Emotional intelligence is the ability to recognize, understand, and manage your own emotions while also recognizing, understanding, and constructively responding to the emotions of others. In the context of adjusting, it allows you to stay grounded during tense phone calls, read between the lines of a client's frustration, and respond with clarity when your patience is tested.

It's not about being soft; it's about being steady. Emotional intelligence helps you maintain a calm center amidst chaos, and that calm often sets the tone for the entire interaction.

THE MORNING EVERYTHING WENT SIDEWAYS

The day began with a denied water claim and a policy-holder who exploded before I could finish my second sentence. I stayed on the line, listening through the shouting and doing my best to remain steady, even though I could feel my chest tightening. My impulse was to match the energy—raise my voice, shut it down, and protect myself. But I didn't. I took a breath. I said, "I hear how frustrating this has been. I want to walk you through what happened, and I'll stay on with you until it makes sense."

Eventually, the volume decreased. We navigated through the explanation. It wasn't perfect—but we managed to get through it.

Two hours later, I was on another call, and a contractor challenged my scope line by line, growing increasingly condescending. By the time I ended that conversation, I could feel my mood slipping. My notes became sharper, my tone flatter, and my attention more scattered.

That afternoon, I found myself snapping at a teammate over a simple question. That's when I realized—I wasn't regulating anymore. I was reacting.

I stepped away for fifteen minutes, without my laptop or phone. Only breath and stillness surrounded me. When I returned, I took ownership. I apologized to my teammate and rewrote the last two notes to express less frustration than I had intended.

That day taught me that emotional intelligence isn't about remaining unbothered. It's about recognizing when the weight is too heavy—and taking action before it seeps into the rest of your work.

The Adjuster's Emotional Landscape

Every day, you may encounter grief, anger, fear, confusion, and disappointment—and those emotions don't just belong to the claimant. They belong to you, too. Whether you're aware of it or not, the emotional weight of this work builds. One harsh conversation may linger. One long day may cloud your clarity. One unfair accusation may shake your confidence.

Emotional intelligence doesn't mean ignoring your emotions; it means recognizing them early enough to prevent them from steering the conversation.

It also involves learning how to adjust your emotional posture according to the needs of the moment. A stressed-out policyholder may require reassurance more than answers. A contractor may need to be listened to before receiving corrections. A teammate may need space to vent before regaining focus. When you develop emotional intelligence, you gain access to a broader range of responses—and experience fewer regrets.

Presence Over Performance

Some adjusters try to power through high-pressure interactions by strictly adhering to the script or shielding themselves with formality. However, clients can sense emotional detachment. They want to know you're engaged, not just prepared.

You don't need to mirror the other person's emotions, but you do need to acknowledge them. Sometimes that sounds like: "I can hear that this situation has been frustrating," or, "This isn't easy—I understand how that must feel." A moment of recognition goes further than you might think.

The key is balance: stay connected, but don't carry their emotions. Stay steady, but not stiff. Emotional intelligence helps you access empathy without absorbing distress, allowing you to remain open without losing your boundaries.

And perhaps most importantly—it helps you recover. A challenging morning doesn't have to ruin your afternoon. A difficult file doesn't need to affect your attitude. The more emotionally attuned you are, the more resilient you become.

Building Your Emotional Awareness

You can't lead what you don't notice. Start by paying attention to your patterns. When do you feel triggered? When do you shut down? When do you lose your patience, lean into sarcasm, or become overly apologetic?

Then ask yourself: What was underneath that? What did I need in that moment? More support? More clarity? More space?

Emotional intelligence is a practice—not a personality trait. It's developed through reflection, feedback, and a willingness to grow. Every time you pause, regulate, or recalibrate during a challenging interaction, you're doing more than improving your performance; you're strengthening your leadership.

🔍 End-of-Chapter Reflection

Use these questions to reflect on how your emotions influence your communication and how you might grow your emotional presence on the job.

1. *When do I feel most emotionally grounded—and what helps me stay there when a situation becomes tense or unpredictable?*

2. *How often do I name what I'm feeling during difficult claims—and what might change if I did?*

3. *What would it look like to lead every interaction from emotional steadiness, even when others are reactive?*

Chapter 8

Empathy: Leading Through Human Connection

Insurance adjusting requires technical skill, but it also demands emotional maturity. You're not just managing damaged property or injury reports—you're stepping into someone's disruption. That disruption may be visible—a flooded living room, a totaled car—or invisible, such as grief, shame, or fear.

"Empathy is not agreement—it's the act of showing someone they've been heard."

Regardless of the loss, empathy allows you to lead with more than just process; it enables you to lead with presence.

Empathy is the ability to understand and connect with what someone else is feeling. It doesn't mean you need to fix their emotions or mirror their pain. It simply means you're willing to meet them where they are, without judgment and without retreat. In claims work, this may involve standing in a soaked kitchen with someone who has just lost their sense of security—or listening on the phone as someone vents about the pressure of mounting bills and delayed repairs.

In those moments, empathy is not just helpful—it is vital.

THE LEADERSHIP SHIFT I DIDN'T EXPECT

I used to think leadership was about decision-making, authority, and getting things right while completing tasks. But one day, I listened to a recorded call from a newer adjuster who had handled a policyholder on the verge of a breakdown. The file had been flagged due to the length of the call—almost 45 minutes for a simple denial. I expected to hear someone floundering and unsure of how to close.

Instead, I heard mastery.

The adjuster never raised their voice, never rushed the caller, and never made promises they couldn't keep. They listened, paraphrased, and paused. When the policyholder said, "I feel like nobody cares," the adjuster responded, "It makes sense that you'd feel that way—it's a hard situation, and you've had to chase a lot of answers. Let me walk you through where we are and what's next."

No theatrics. No scripts. Just grounded, human leadership.

That call ended with the policyholder saying thank you—not because the decision changed, but because the tone did. That day, I realized that leadership in adjusting doesn't always look like strength; sometimes it looks like softness that knows how to stand firm. Sometimes it sounds like empathy spoken with clarity, and sometimes, that's the hardest—and most powerful—thing to lead with.

The Power of Feeling Seen

Empathy fosters connection. It conveys to the person on the other end of the line that their experience matters—that they're not just another case or claim number but a human being navigating loss, confusion, or disruption.

For many policyholders, you are the first real person they encounter after something goes wrong. Perhaps they've come home to find a collapsed ceiling. Maybe their vehicle was rear-ended—with kids in the back seat. Perhaps they're recovering from surgery and trying to understand a confusing medical claim. These moments are emotionally charged, and the words you choose—or the pauses you offer—can either calm or inflame.

Empathy might sound like, "That sounds incredibly frustrating—let's figure out the next step together."

It might look like giving space before you speak, slowing your tone, and choosing curiosity over control.

You don't have to absorb their stress. And you don't have to pretend to understand every detail of their experience. But you do need to show that you're willing to acknowledge their reality, rather than rush past it.

Barriers to Empathy in Claims Work

There are many reasons why empathy can get lost. Perhaps you have experienced five difficult calls in a row. Maybe you feel pressured to close files quickly. You might also be emotionally drained from a week of escalations. In such moments, it's easy to switch to auto-pilot—merely checking boxes, answering questions, and keeping conversations transactional.

But when you operate in that mode too often, people stop feeling seen. Even if your information is correct, the interaction feels cold. This subtle shift gets noticed—and it often appears later in complaints, poor reviews, or breakdowns in cooperation.

Some adjusters avoid empathy because they confuse it with agreement. However, empathy doesn't equate to surrender. You can express understanding without altering your decision. You can acknowledge pain without compromising boundaries. Empathy is not about conceding—it's about leading with clarity and care.

Practicing Empathy Without Burnout

Empathy is not emotional absorption. You are not required to carry every story you hear. The best adjusters learn to remain emotionally available without becoming emotionally drained. They find a rhythm that enables them to care deeply while still protecting their capacity.

This is where boundaries work with empathy—not against it.

You can say, "I understand how hard this is," without stepping into their stress. You can say, "Here's what I can do next," without overpromising. You can hold space without carrying the weight.

Empathy transforms into a form of leadership when paired with emotional discipline. When combined with the skills you've developed throughout this book—listening, questioning, documentation, presence—it distinguishes between surviving this work and truly transforming it.

Because, at its core, empathy isn't about being nice; it's about being real, grounded, and responsive. It's about leading from your humanity—without losing it.

🔍 End-of-Chapter Reflection

Use these questions to explore how you practice empathy and how you can build stronger connection in emotionally charged moments.

1. *When was the last time someone truly felt heard by me— and what did I do differently in that moment?*

2. *Where am I at risk of becoming emotionally numb in my role, and how can I reconnect without burning out?*

3. *How can I show more empathy in my next five conversations—without losing my clarity or professional boundaries?*

Chapter 9

Leading Through Communication and Ownership

Insurance adjusting is, at its core, relationship-driven work. From policyholders to contractors, team leads to carrier contacts, every part of your role depends on how well you communicate with people—especially under pressure. However, technical accuracy isn't sufficient. It's your interpersonal skills—your emotional posture, tone, timing, and presence—that determine how people respond to you and how you lead each file to completion.

"This is the work before the title. Ownership is the beginning of leadership."

Interpersonal communication is more than just being polite. It involves navigating tension, resetting unproductive conversations, and building trust with individuals who may be reactive, overwhelmed, or oppositional. When executed effectively, it becomes your strongest leadership tool.

But what turns communication into leadership is ownership.

Ownership means you don't just interact—you take responsibility. You don't just speak—you guide. You don't just pass along information—you stand behind it. And in moments where communication becomes strained or decisions are difficult, ownership is what separates competent adjusters from transformational ones.

THE MOMENT I REALIZED IT WAS MINE TO FIX

I was wrapping up my fourth claim of the day when a teammate pinged me: "Policyholder on line three says she's been through three adjusters already. Needs someone to 'actually do something.'"

I was tempted to punt. The file was messy—scattered documentation, conflicting notes, and no clear next steps. I could've responded, "Not my claim," or "She needs to speak with the desk team." But something in me paused. I could hear the fatigue in her voice when I picked up. She wasn't just frustrated—she was exhausted. And honestly, so was I.

Still, I said, "I know this hasn't been smooth. I'm going to take the lead on this now, and I'll be your point of contact from here on out."

I didn't have all the answers in that moment. But I had presence. I had enough steadiness to reset the tone, clarify the path forward, and follow through. Three days later, she emailed my supervisor—not to praise the settlement, but to say, "He actually took ownership."

That changed how I approached every claim afterward. Not because it made things easier—but because it made me better. I stopped hiding behind protocol and started leading with clarity. I realized that leadership didn't come from a title—it came from how I chose to show up in the difficult moments.

The Daily Dynamics of Leading Through Relationships

Every conversation in this work is unique. One moment may require compassion and patience; the next may demand boundary-setting and firmness. A contractor might challenge your scope. A policyholder could be reeling from an unexpected denial. A colleague may feel stressed, fall behind, or lack clarity. Your ability to read the moment and adjust your tone defines your influence.

When interpersonal communication is strong, trust is fostered—even when the outcome is challenging. Conversely, when communication is weak, tension persists, and conversations become mired in reactivity or defensiveness.

Great adjusters know how to reset a room, even over the phone. They recognize when emotion clouds logic—and rather than fueling it, they ground it. That's not just emotional intelligence; that's leadership.

Navigating Disagreement Without Losing Direction

Disagreement is a natural aspect of claims work. Not everyone will agree with your decision. Not every contractor will appreciate your scope. And not every colleague will perceive the situation the same way you do.

Leadership in communication involves learning how to disagree with clarity and care. It entails choosing to reframe instead of react. It means saying, "Let's walk through what's been done and what's possible now," rather than defaulting to blame, avoidance, or over-explaining.

It also means holding space for disagreement without internalizing it. You can take feedback without crumbling. You can acknowledge someone's frustration without necessarily agreeing with it. Ownership means drawing the line when necessary—but doing so with professionalism, not pride.

Claim Ownership as a Mindset

You don't need a title to lead in this work. Leadership in adjusting isn't measured by rank or authority—it's measured by presence. It's about how you show up when clarity is absent, when tensions are high, and when responsibility is too easily overlooked. Ownership is not about taking control of everything—it's about becoming the person who sees things through when others don't.

Sometimes, that means taking accountability for follow-up, even when someone else dropped the ball. It means being the voice that re-centers the process when things go sideways—not to point fingers, but to move the claim forward. Other times, it means choosing to clarify communication that was muddled before you arrived. Even if it's not your mess, you become the one who brings calm and direction.

Owning a claim can also mean being the one to make the hard call—when everyone else is hesitant, when no one wants to be the one to say no, or when the decision will not be popular. It doesn't mean rushing to closure. It means moving with intention, weighing the facts, and making a choice that holds up under pressure.

Claiming ownership is not about getting everything right. It's not about knowing everything. It's about refusing to hide behind excuses, protocol, or silence. It's about staying committed to finding the right answer—ethically, thoroughly, and with professionalism—because the claim deserves it. And because your name is on it.

From Communicator to Leader

The adjusters who rise are not always the fastest or the most experienced. They are the ones who lead with steadiness when others shrink back. They own their files as they own their name. They make decisions with both clarity and humility. They understand that interpersonal strength and internal integrity are not separate—they are the same skill in different forms.

You don't build a leadership brand overnight. You develop it through the quiet, daily choices of how you speak, how you listen, how you follow through, and how you maintain your principles. When your communication style aligns with your sense of ownership, you become someone others trust to lead—not just to respond.

🔍 End-of-Chapter Reflection

Use these questions to reflect on your interpersonal presence and your willingness to take full ownership—especially when it's uncomfortable.

1. **When was the last time I took full ownership of a difficult interaction—and how did that change the outcome or relationship?**

2. **What conversations in my workflow tend to trigger avoidance or passivity—and how can I meet them with more leadership?**

3. **What would it look like to communicate in a way that consistently reflects clarity, confidence, and accountability?**

Chapter 10

Conflict Resolution and Problem-Solving

Conflict is not a sign that something has gone wrong. In insurance adjusting, it's often an indication that something significant is at stake: a coverage decision, a financial outcome, or an unmet expectation. The presence of tension doesn't signal failure; it indicates friction surrounding something important. What matters most isn't whether conflict arises—it's how you manage it when it does.

"The real goal isn't to win the argument—it's to preserve the relationship while resolving the issue."

Nearly every claim carries the potential for disagreement. A policyholder challenges the estimate. A contractor disputes the scope. A colleague questions your assessment. These moments are inevitable—they come with the territory. But how you handle them whether the outcome is a breakdown or a breakthrough.

When you approach conflict with steadiness rather than defensiveness, you transition from reaction to leadership. You safeguard the relationship while steering the claim—and the conversation—toward resolution.

THE PUSHBACK I DIDN'T SEE COMING

It was supposed to be a simple follow-up. I called the contractor to review a denied supplement and expected a short, professional exchange. Instead, I was met with hostility. "This is the third time your firm has lowballed this job," he snapped. "It's like no one's actually reading the scope."

I felt my chest tighten. My first instinct was to defend the decision, to explain the estimate line by line. But something in his tone stopped me. This wasn't just about pricing; it was about feeling unheard.

I paused and said, "It sounds like this has been frustrating—and that this isn't the first time it's happened. Walk me through what you're seeing from your side."

He did. And while the final outcome didn't change, the energy shifted. The aggression transformed into collaboration. We clarified several misalignments and agreed to maintain closer contact going forward.

That call reminded me that conflict isn't always about disagreement—it's often about disconnect. And resolution doesn't always come from proving your point. Sometimes, it starts by simply creating space for someone else to be heard.

Why Conflict Feels Personal

Many people avoid conflict because they associate it with hostility, loss of control, or personal attack. However, most workplace tension doesn't stem from bad intent—it arises from misalignment. Two people trying to meet different needs, two timelines pulling in opposite directions, and two expectations that were never clearly communicated.

In claims adjusting, the stakes are emotional. Clients are under stress. Deadlines are real. The pressure to do it right—quickly, compliantly, and compassionately—can feel overwhelming. When that pressure isn't acknowledged or managed, it spills over. It affects tone, documentation, and the subtle ways we communicate with and about one another.

Understanding that conflict is often a symptom—not the cause—provides access to a different kind of response. One rooted not in fear, but in clarity.

From Escalation to Resolution

Conflict resolution begins not with your strategy, but with your posture. If you enter a conversation ready to win, defend, or convince, you're likely to miss what is truly being asked of you. However, if you lead with curiosity—if you stay grounded even when others escalate—you can reset the entire tone.

Great adjusters don't avoid tension. They face it with calm presence and clear language. They don't bulldoze through disagreements, nor do they shy away from them. They ask clarifying questions, validate what's real, and steer the conversation toward clarity, even when resolution takes time.

It doesn't always mean changing your answer. Sometimes, the answer is still no. However, a clear no—delivered with respect and reason—builds far more trust than a vague yes that leads to confusion.

How you manage the space between disagreement and decision is where your leadership shows.

Problem-Solving Under Pressure

Once the emotional charge of conflict begins to settle, one question remains: What now?

Problem-solving is the process of moving from conflict to closure. It's not about finding the perfect solution immediately. It's about your willingness to stay engaged, remain professional, and keep moving until the next right step becomes clear.

Sometimes, problem-solving means taking a moment to review the file with fresh eyes. Other times, it involves bringing in a peer or supervisor. It may also require calling the policyholder back after confirming the guidelines. The point is, problem-solving is not about having the answer on demand; it's about demonstrating your commitment to finding it.

People remember how they felt during conflict. But they remember even more whether you followed through. Did you close the loop? Did you communicate the next steps clearly? Did you stay engaged—even after the tension faded?

The adjusters who stand out are not those who avoid conflict. They are the ones who transform conflict into clarity and then turn that clarity into action.

🔍 End-of-Chapter Reflection

Use these questions to reflect on how you respond to conflict—and how you can lead through it instead of reacting to it.

1. **When faced with tension or disagreement, do I tend to avoid, escalate, or approach it calmly? What's behind that pattern?**

2. **How can I become more curious when someone challenges my decision, instead of immediately defending it?**

3. **What would it look like to become the person others trust to solve—not just manage—problems under pressure?**

Chapter 11

Dealing with Difficult Clients and Situations

No matter how clear your explanation, how fair your settlement, or how calm your tone—some conversations will still be challenging. Some clients will continue to push back. And some situations will test the very limits of your professionalism, patience, and emotional regulation.

"Sometimes the claim isn't what's being contested—it's the feeling of being dismissed."

This is not a failure. It's the nature of the work.

As an adjuster, you often enter people's lives during moments of stress, disruption, or financial uncertainty. Emotions run high. Expectations are not always realistic. And outcomes—regardless of how compliant or well-explained—may fall short of what the client hoped for. In those moments, you are doing more than explaining policy; you are managing emotion. Sometimes, that emotion is directed not at the claim, but at you.

Learning to navigate these interactions isn't about becoming emotionally numb. It's about becoming emotionally steady. It's about knowing what's yours to carry, and what's not—while still offering clarity and composure to someone who may be angry, overwhelmed, or in pain.

THE CALL THAT NEARLY BROKE ME

It was the end of a long day, and I was trying to close one last file before logging off. The claim itself was straightforward: water damage was denied due to wear and tear. All the documentation supported the decision. I dialed the policyholder to walk them through it.

What I didn't expect was the wave of emotion on the other end of the line. "You people are all the same," he said, his voice rising. "You deny claims just to hit your quotas. You don't care that we're living in a disaster zone."

I could feel my jaw tighten. I hadn't even finished my first sentence. Part of me wanted to defend myself—to remind him that I wasn't responsible for the policy language. Another part just wanted to end the call and document "client noncooperative."

But something told me to pause.

I took a slow breath and said, "I can hear how stressful this has been. I'd like to walk you through what's in the file, and we can talk through any questions you have together."

The yelling didn't stop right away, but the tone began to shift—slowly. Eventually, we had a real conversation—not a perfect one, but a calmer one. By the end, he thanked me, not because he agreed, but because I didn't fight him back.

That call reminded me that sometimes, the claim isn't what's being contested—it's the feeling of being ignored, dismissed, or powerless. And that's where presence matters most.

Recognizing What's Beneath the Surface

Difficult behavior often signals—not merely symptoms. Anger can conceal fear. Repetition may indicate confusion. Hostility might stem from helplessness. By recognizing this, you can steer the conversation instead of merely reacting to it.

Not every client is combative—some are simply desperate. Others may be grieving or emotionally flooded and lack the language to express it productively. Your job isn't to absorb their emotion or excuse poor behavior. It's to anchor the conversation in clarity and calm, even when the waves are high.

Asking yourself quietly, "What's really going on here?" can change everything. It provides you distance from the trigger and helps you focus on what's being asked—not just what's being said.

Staying Grounded When You're Triggered

Some moments will catch you off guard: a passive-aggressive tone, a sharp insult, a sudden outburst. It's human to feel emotion in those moments—but your role is not to suppress those feelings; it's to manage them wisely.

Grounding begins long before the call starts. It involves how you prepare between files and how you recover after challenging conversations. In the moment, grounding may appear as slowing your breath before responding or taking a silent pause to reset your posture and tone.

You don't need to match intensity to prove authority. You don't need to rush to fix things or soften your decision just to de-escalate. Sometimes, a simple phrase like, "I can hear your frustration, and I want to stay focused on what's possible," can do more to stabilize the moment than any technical answer.

Your power doesn't come from control; it comes from composure. It stems from the ability to redirect without escalating, to remain anchored while emotions swirl.

Protecting Your Boundaries Without Losing Your Humanity

Boundaries are not barriers; they are bridges to professionalism. They allow you to remain human without being consumed.

You can care deeply and still say, "I can't continue the conversation if the tone becomes disrespectful."

You can listen with empathy and still say, "If needed, I'll follow up in writing after this call."

These aren't scripts; they're signals. They show that you're willing to stay in the conversation, but not at the cost of your dignity or theirs. Boundaries protect your emotional bandwidth and the integrity of the claims process.

The goal isn't to be unshakable; it's to be responsive, not reactive; consistent, not cold; firm, but fair. This balance allows you to be the steady presence people need when the conversation starts to unravel—and the fair guide they'll remember when it's resolved.

🔍 End-of-Chapter Reflection

Use these questions to assess how you handle high-emotion situations and where you can build greater steadiness under stress.

1. *What behaviors or tones tend to trigger me—and how do I typically respond in those moments?*

2. *Where have I let someone's energy shift my own—and what could I do differently to stay grounded?*

3. *What would it look like to protect both my boundaries and my humanity in every difficult interaction?*

Part III

Operational & Professional Mastery

Soft skills involve not only how you connect with others but also how you manage yourself. In the fast-paced, emotionally complex world of insurance adjusting, your success relies as much on your ability to stay organized, focused, and ethically grounded as it does on your communication or conflict resolution skills.

This section shifts the lens inward. It's about the invisible foundation of professionalism—the habits and decisions that enable you to perform well under pressure without burning out. Operational mastery is what converts stress into structure and high volume into a sustainable workflow.

You'll explore how to prioritize your workload without losing clarity, how to set realistic goals while managing shifting deadlines, and how to navigate those challenging file days without letting your emotions take over. You'll also learn how to collaborate across teams to avoid miscommunication, how to uphold legal and regulatory standards under scrutiny, and how to lead ethically—even when no one's watching.

These upcoming chapters focus not on perfection but on consistency. They emphasize the importance of choosing self-respect over speed and clarity over chaos. Professionalism is not something you claim; it's something you prove, day after day, file after file.

When pressure mounts and pace quickens, operational excellence serves as your anchor. This section will help you secure that anchor with confidence.

Chapter 12

Time Management

Time is one of the most valuable—and limited—resources in insurance adjusting. With inspections to schedule, reports to write, policyholders to follow up with, and supervisors expecting timely documentation, managing time isn't just about productivity; it's about sustainability. It requires protecting your clarity, mental bandwidth, and professional reputation in the face of nonstop demand.

> *"Time management is emotional management. When you lose your rhythm, you lose your edge."*

In claims work, the clock never stops ticking. Deadlines loom. Voicemails stack up. Files reopen. And just when you start catching up, a surge hits—or a new carrier request drops into your queue. Without a clear system or personal rhythm, it's easy to slip into reactive mode—putting out fires instead of leading the process.

Time management in this field isn't about perfect color-coded calendars or rigid routines. It's about building the ability to prioritize under pressure, stay present amid distractions, and reset quickly when the day throws you off track.

> ## WHEN URGENCY HIJACKED MY DAY
>
> I once spent an entire afternoon chasing a single file—back-to-back calls, photo requests, follow-up notes, and clarifications with the contractor—fully immersed in the urgency of the moment. It wasn't until 5:12 p.m. that my supervisor flagged four compliance deadlines I'd missed, and I realized I had let noise override priority.
>
> That day changed everything. I stopped managing my time based on who was shouting the loudest. I started managing it by impact. Urgency is loud, but importance is quiet. You only hear it when you slow down long enough to listen.

Urgency vs. Importance

Not every urgent task is important, and not every important task feels urgent. One of the most powerful time management skills is learning to separate the two.

The client who has called three times today may be loud, but that doesn't mean they are the most pressing. A silent file nearing a regulatory deadline may carry far more weight. High-performing adjusters develop the ability to zoom out, assess their caseload from above, and prioritize based on risk, impact, and sequence—not noise.

This doesn't mean you should ignore people or postpone callbacks indefinitely. It means you should organize your response in a way that preserves your ability to serve everyone—not just the person who happens to be demanding the most attention at that moment.

Planning Around Reality

Effective time management in adjusting isn't idealistic—it's realistic. It accounts for chaos. Roofs will be inaccessible. Contractors will cancel last minute. A call that should have taken ten minutes will stretch to forty-five. The best adjusters don't plan for perfection. They plan for what's likely.

That means building flexibility into your day. It means identifying your "must-do" items before the rest of your calendar fills in. It means protecting the time for what absolutely needs to happen—critical documentation, regulatory responses, policyholder communication—before adding everything else in.

Planning isn't about creating a rigid script. It's about resetting your clarity so you can move through your day with purpose. Whether you use a digital task list, a sticky note system, or a morning reset routine, the tool matters less than the intention behind it: getting clear before getting caught up.

Reclaiming Your Focus

Distraction is one of the stealthiest time thieves—and one of the hardest to notice until the day is gone. The constant ping of emails, the temptation to multitask, and the habit of jumping between systems or conversations all chip away at your attention, stamina, and ability to finish anything completely.

But the adjusters who manage their time best aren't always working harder—they're working smarter. They batch similar tasks, reduce decision fatigue, and focus on one action at a time. They recognize which parts of their workflow require full attention and protect those periods from interruption.

Just as importantly, they know how to return to center when they've drifted. They don't lose the entire day to a single detour. They recognize the signals—spiraling, irritability, avoidance—and they pause, recalibrate, and return to tasks with sharper awareness.

Time management is not solely about efficiency; it encompasses leadership. It involves the leadership of your attention, your energy, and your decisions. In this domain, it serves as one of the most crucial predictors of long-term success—not merely in completed tasks but also in sustained well-being.

🔍 End-of-Chapter Reflection

Use these questions to evaluate how you're currently managing time—and where you can lead yourself more clearly through your day.

1. *When do I feel most in control of my day—and what patterns help me get there?*

2. *Where am I losing time to distraction, avoidance, or low-value tasks that drain my energy?*

3. *If I led my calendar with clarity and confidence, what would need to shift—starting today?*

Chapter 13

Goals, Deadlines, and Workload

In insurance adjusting, goals aren't optional—they're everywhere. Whether set by leadership, driven by carrier expectations, or self-imposed in the name of progress, they shape your daily experience. Deadlines define your rhythm, while volume drives your urgency.

"You can't solve pressure with willpower alone. You need a system that protects your energy."

Together, they form the framework that either keeps you moving or pushes you to the edge.

Managing workload in this field isn't merely about checking boxes. It's about maintaining focus when the pace picks up. It's about establishing realistic targets, not just reactive ones. And it's about understanding how to meet expectations without constantly depleting your reserves.

Industry Insight: According to a 2023 McKinsey & Company study, professionals who engage in structured workload planning are 28 percent more likely to meet deadlines and 40 percent less likely to report burnout symptoms.

THE COST OF OVERLOAD

The insurance industry is no stranger to performance pressure. A 2021 Deloitte study found that over 50 percent of claims professionals report feeling burned out at least once per quarter—often due to high volume, a lack of clarity around expectations, or unrealistic performance metrics.

Another survey by the Insurance Information Institute revealed that claims cycle times have increased by 13–18 percent during high-volume years, placing additional strain on frontline adjusters who are tasked with balancing speed and accuracy. When deadlines are missed, it's not just a performance issue—it becomes a trust issue with policyholders and internal teams alike.

Workload mismanagement is one of the fastest ways to erode morale and drive turnover. However, it doesn't have to be unavoidable. Adjusters who learn to manage performance with intention, rather than pressure, create a more sustainable impact—and often achieve better results.

Setting Goals That Actually Work

A goal is only as useful as the system that supports it. When adjusting, that system must be flexible enough to adapt to the unexpected, yet structured enough to maintain progress when decisions accumulate.

Effective goals are clear, measurable, and grounded in reality. This means defining not just what needs to happen—but when, how, and in what order. Daily and weekly targets help bring focus to large caseloads, but they also require regular review. What worked last month may not work during a surge. What's realistic on paper may become overwhelming after a difficult policyholder call or a tech issue in the field.

When goals are set with intention, they serve as a stabilizer. Conversely, when they're set arbitrarily or not revisited, they can create additional pressure.

Deadlines as Anchors—Not Weapons

Deadlines can be beneficial. They provide structure and promote decision-making. However, they can also become emotional flashpoints—especially when they are unclear, unrealistic, or conflict with real-time events.

Adjusters working in siloed or high-pressure teams often face misaligned expectations: "Close faster," "Document more thoroughly," "Respond within the hour." Without clarity, these become competing goals—and that's when frustration builds.

Strong professionals don't just chase deadlines—they clarify them. They ask, "What's truly urgent?" "What's driving this timeline?" "How can I keep momentum without sacrificing accuracy?" When deadlines are treated as guides rather than threats, they promote focus rather than fear.

Managing Volume Without Losing Control

High workload is part of adjusting, but unmanaged volume leads to reactivity, burnout, and mistakes. The key isn't to escape pressure; it's to build systems that help you carry it with control.

This might look like:

- Blocking time each day to close files instead of only reacting to incoming calls
- Protecting your energy by scheduling lower-emotion tasks after high-stress ones
- Creating a simple tracking method for outstanding items to reduce mental load

Research Insight: A 2023 study by McKinsey found that professionals who batch tasks and pre-plan transitions between work types report a 23 percent increase in task completion and a 40 percent decrease in perceived burnout compared to those who multitask continuously.

In this environment, clarity isn't a luxury—it's a survival tool.

Sustainable Performance Is Strategic

You cannot solve workload pressure with willpower alone; you need a strategy. This involves aligning your daily efforts with meaningful goals. It also entails resetting your targets when conditions change. Additionally, it means refusing to let urgency become your only compass.

The adjusters who thrive long-term aren't always the ones with the highest close rates; they are the ones who lead themselves with discipline, protect their clarity, and view performance as a process, not a sprint.

🔍 End-of-Chapter Reflection

Use these questions to evaluate how you currently manage your workload—and how you can align your goals and deadlines with long-term sustainability.

1. *When do my goals feel like stabilizers—and when do they start to feel like pressure points?*

2. *Where am I allowing urgency to drive decisions at the cost of strategy or sustainability?*

3. *What one shift in my planning, pacing, or prioritization could reduce daily stress without reducing performance?*

Chapter 14

Teamwork

Insurance adjusting may appear to be an independent role, but the reality is far more interconnected. Whether you're in the field or at a desk, managing catastrophe claims or working in a centralized unit, your success depends on how well you collaborate with others.

"Leadership in adjusting doesn't require a team of direct reports—it requires the courage to set a steady tone."

Teamwork in adjusting doesn't always require brainstorming sessions or shared case reviews. More often, it manifests in the seamless handoff between departments, the accuracy of your notes for the next adjuster, the tone of your email when a supervisor is under pressure, or the patience you offer a colleague when you're stretched thin.

Data Insight: According to a 2022 McKinsey report, teams that demonstrate consistent collaboration outperform their siloed counterparts by over 30 percent in productivity and task resolution. Additionally, research from Harvard Business Review shows that workers who feel supported by their team report 40 percent less burnout—even in high-stress fields like healthcare and insurance.

Field Note: A 2022 Deloitte survey on insurance team performance found that adjusters in high-trust teams resolved claims 35 percent faster and reported significantly higher job satisfaction, regardless of their experience level.

The Unspoken Culture of Your Team

Every team possesses a culture—even if no one discusses it. Some teams feel energized, solution-oriented, and grounded in mutual respect, while others seem transactional, competitive, or disconnected. This culture doesn't originate from mission statements; it is formed by how individuals treat one another during moments of pressure, uncertainty, or transition.

You don't need to be a manager to influence the tone. You shape it every time you communicate clearly, show patience during stressful moments, or respond to a difficult handoff with professionalism instead of resentment.

Teamwork sometimes involves checking in on a colleague who is falling behind. It may require stepping up to cover a file when someone is absent. Additionally, it simply entails refraining from expressing frustration in a way that diminishes the energy of those around you.

Culture isn't created in meetings; it's formed in the margins. Those who take responsibility for these moments often become culture carriers—individuals who enhance the atmosphere of every room they enter, rather than merely managing the mood.

THE TEAM THAT GOT ME THROUGH THE SURGE

I'll never forget the storm surge of my third year in the field. We were drowning in files—over 40 per adjuster, all urgent and emotionally heavy. I was doing my best to stay afloat, but I was slipping. One afternoon, I missed an inspection window and didn't have time to warn the policyholder. The voicemail she left was brutal.

Before I could spiral, one of my teammates entered my cubicle with two bottles of water and a Post-it note. On it, he'd written: "I've got your outbound for the next hour. Go reset."

I didn't ask. He just noticed.

That moment changed how I viewed teamwork. It is not about getting everything right—it is about presence. It is about noticing. And it is about being the kind of teammate who makes pressure more bearable—because they choose to share it with you, not throw it back at you.

Collaboration vs. Competition

In a performance-driven environment like insurance, it's easy to slip into quiet competition. Metrics matter. Close rates are tracked. Recognition is real. But when competition becomes your only guide, you begin to view teammates as threats instead of collaborators.

Industry Research: The University of Michigan found that "high-performance" cultures rooted in comparison have a 53 percent greater turnover rate than collaborative teams with shared accountability structures. Why? Because people stop sharing, hide mistakes, and hoard knowledge.

But collaboration doesn't dilute excellence—it amplifies it. Sharing insights, helping someone troubleshoot, mentoring a new hire—these aren't distractions; they are how strong departments are built.

The best adjusters understand this. They protect their own productivity, but they don't do it at the expense of others. They share what they've learned and take pride in raising the standard, not just their stats. They know that every time they contribute, the entire system gets stronger.

Being a Team Player Without Losing Yourself

Being collaborative doesn't mean complying with everything. Strong team players establish boundaries. They provide honest feedback. They know how to say no gracefully and how to offer support without overextending themselves.

You can challenge ideas without undermining others. You can care for others without taking on their responsibilities. You can be available without feeling depleted.

Teamwork thrives when people understand who you are, what you contribute, and where your boundaries lie. This clarity fosters trust, and trust accelerates progress—especially in high-pressure situations.

When you work in a team built on mutual respect, tough days remain challenging, but they do not become breaking points. Regardless of whether you're officially leading that team, you are contributing to its tone in practice.

🔍 End-of-Chapter Reflection

Use these questions to reflect on how you contribute to your team—and how you can strengthen your presence, support, and influence within it.

1. **What tone do I bring into the team space—and how does that shape our shared culture?**

2. **Where could I be more collaborative or supportive without overextending myself?**

3. **What would it look like to be a team member who balances clarity, boundaries, and presence in high-pressure settings?**

Chapter 15

Navigating Legal and Regulatory Issues

Insurance adjusting sits at the intersection of people, policy, and the law. Every file you touch is bound not only by internal guidelines and client expectations, but also by the legal and regulatory frameworks that govern what you can say, decide, and document. Whether

"Compliance is more than following rules—it's communicating in ways that stand up to scrutiny."

you're handling a routine water loss or navigating a complex liability claim, your legal literacy protects not just your company but also your credibility.

At first glance, the legal side of adjusting may feel procedural—something you do to stay within bounds or check a compliance box. However, in reality, legal alignment is foundational to your professional reputation. It shapes how you write, how you speak, and how you manage ambiguity. What seems like a small omission or an overly casual phrase can later become the very thing a regulator or legal team scrutinizes.

The good news? Legal fluency doesn't require a law degree. It necessitates consistency, clarity, and a deep respect for the boundaries and responsibilities inherent in your role.

Professionalism Is Legal Protection

You don't need to be a lawyer to adjust a claim, but you must understand the legal implications of your documentation, communication, and decisions.

According to the National Association of Insurance Commissioners (NAIC), documentation quality is among the top three factors leading to regulatory complaints and file reviews. In over 60 percent of disputed claims that escalate to legal or regulatory action, adjuster communication or vague file notes are cited as contributing factors.

That means every claim note you write, every decision you recommend, and every call you log—all contribute to a legal narrative. Your documentation doesn't just show what happened; it shows how it happened, who was involved, what was known, what was said, and when.

The difference between writing, "Client lied about damage," versus, "Client's statements on 3/12 and 3/15 about the cause of loss were inconsistent," is the difference between opinion and evidence. In legal review, that distinction matters.

A LESSON IN LEGAL PRECISION

Years ago, I managed a theft claim in which the policyholder reported missing items two weeks after the alleged loss. I took notes diligently, documented the interview, and recommended denial due to late reporting and insufficient documentation.

Six months later, the claim resurfaced. A lawyer took on the case, arguing mishandling and miscommunication. My file was pulled for audit.

One of my early notes read: *"Client appears dishonest. Delay in reporting raises red flags."* I remember writing that after a frustrating call, convinced I was capturing the tone of the interaction.

That one sentence became the focus of the dispute. Not the photos. Not the timeline. That note.

What I intended as shorthand became a liability. It taught me that even accurate instincts must be framed with professionalism and neutrality. Since then, I have never written a subjective phrase without asking: Would I be comfortable reading this in court?

Know Your Role—And Your Boundaries

One of the most important aspects of legal alignment is understanding your authority. You may be authorized to assess damage, suggest scope, or interpret policy language—but not to make unilateral decisions regarding coverage, subrogation, or liability.

Well-intentioned statements like, "You should be covered for that," or "That won't be a problem," can create false expectations and compliance risk. In a legal or regulatory setting, ambiguity is vulnerability.

Strong adjusters understand when to pause, when to escalate, and when to say, "Let me confirm that before I give you a definitive answer." Confidence is not about always knowing; it's about knowing when to verify.

In fact, a study published by the Insurance Research Council (IRC) found that claims involving unauthorized commitments or coverage misstatements were 2.4 times more likely to be disputed or to result in partial reversals during litigation or complaint resolution.

Compliance Is a Culture—Not Just a Checklist

Regulatory and legal awareness should not reside solely in training binders or annual quizzes. It should be ingrained in your team culture. When compliance is regarded as a shared value—not merely an obligation—it transforms how teams operate. It fosters clarity. It minimizes errors. And it equips individuals with the language to speak up when something doesn't feel right.

In high-performing organizations, compliance isn't something to dodge. It's something to respect. That shows in how carefully adjusters document, how often they ask for policy clarification, and how consistently they update their understanding as carrier guidelines or regulations evolve.

And while you may not set the rules, you do set the tone. The way you speak, write, and respond to ambiguity either reinforces compliance or erodes it.

Staying Teachable in a Changing Landscape

Laws change. Regulations shift. Carrier guidelines are updated more frequently than most people realize. Staying legally aligned doesn't require obsessing over every update; it requires remaining teachable.

This involves attending update briefings, reading internal bulletins, asking questions when something feels unclear, and treating every policy—no matter how familiar—as a contract, not a conversation.

Professionalism is not static. In a legal environment, even well-meaning shortcuts can backfire. The best adjusters do not merely protect the claim; they protect themselves by document-ing professionally and communicating with clarity that withstands scrutiny.

🔍 End-of-Chapter Reflection

Use these questions to assess your relationship to the legal and regulatory side of your work—and where you can grow in confidence and clarity.

1. **How confident do I feel in understanding the legal framework behind the claims I handle—and where might I need more clarity?**

2. **Do my notes and decisions reflect factual, neutral documentation—or do I sometimes slip into assumptions or vague language?**

3. **What's one way I can become more proactive in staying aligned with the legal and compliance expectations in my role?**

Chapter 16

Navigating Ethical Dilemmas in Adjusting

In theory, doing the right thing should be simple. In practice, it often isn't.

Insurance adjusting occupies the intersection of people, policy, money, and emotion. This creates fertile ground for ethical tension. You may be asked to prioritize speed over thoroughness. You may feel subtle pressure to interpret a gray area in favor of your employer. You may hear an unsettling comment in a meeting—and have to decide whether to speak up or stay silent.

"Ethical leadership doesn't wait for an audience. It shows up when no one's watching."

The most challenging ethical dilemmas are rarely dramatic; they arrive quietly. They manifest in how you write a file note, how you explain a denial, or how you respond to a subtle nudge to "just get it closed." In those moments, your ethical leadership is revealed—not just by what you do but by how grounded you are in what you believe.

THE NOTE I CHOSE NOT TO WRITE

I once shadowed a colleague on a high-value property claim. The policyholder's story had a few holes, and the damage looked... convenient. As we left the inspection, my colleague said, "We both know this claim's a stretch. I'll write it up to fit—it's not worth a fight."

I paused. I knew she meant well. I also knew what she meant by "fit."

Later that day, she asked me to draft the preliminary note. My cursor hovered for a long time. I didn't want to offend her. I didn't want to escalate anything unnecessarily. But I also couldn't bring myself to frame the story in a way that felt misleading.

Instead, I wrote what I saw. I noted inconsistencies factually. I added photographs. And I chose not to assume intent. When she reviewed it, she simply said, "Thanks for handling that."

No fallout. No drama. But that day stayed with me—not because of the claim, but because I realized that ethics isn't always about grand gestures. Sometimes, it's about what you don't write. What you don't agree to. And what you quietly protect—even when no one else would have noticed if you didn't.

When Integrity Feels Inconvenient

In fast-paced, adjusting environments, ethical choices aren't always easy—or rewarded. Choosing the high road might involve asking more questions when the team seeks answers. It might require slowing down a decision that others are ready to finalize. It might mean being the only one uncomfortable in a room filled with silence.

But ethical leadership isn't about comfort. It's about courage.

According to a 2022 study by the Ethics & Compliance Initiative (ECI), nearly 59 percent of employees in high-regulation industries like insurance face pressure to compromise ethical standards at some point in their careers. Those who received ethics training and felt supported by leadership were twice as likely to report concerns—and far less likely to engage in misconduct.

In other words, culture matters—but so does individual courage. And in the field, you won't always have a compliance officer nearby. You are the first and last line of ethical decision-making.

The Gray Areas No One Talks About

Ethical tension rarely arrives with a red flag. It arrives in subtle moments:

- When someone says, *"Let's just code it that way—it'll go through faster."*
- Or, *"No need to document that part. It might open a can of worms."*
- Or even, *"That's the guideline, but we don't really follow it unless we have to."*

In these moments, you're not just managing a file; you're managing your values. You're deciding what kind of professional you want to be and setting a precedent for yourself, your team, and your future credibility.

Research shows that ethical "slippage" often starts small. A 2020 article in the Journal of Business Ethics highlights that employees under time pressure are 39 percent more likely to engage in minor ethical compromises if they perceive the shortcut as beneficial to the organization. That intent—while understandable—can still lead to serious consequences if repeated or normalized.

Owning Your Voice and Your Values

Being ethical doesn't mean being perfect. It means being alert. Accountable. Willing to speak with clarity when the easy route would be silence.

Strong adjusters learn how to say:

- *"I'd like to revisit that decision with the file in front of me."*
- *"I want to make sure this aligns with the policy before I move forward."*
- *"Let me confirm that with the team before we communicate anything."*

These statements don't signal doubt; they signal integrity. They demonstrate that you understand your work impacts more than just a close rate; it impacts trust, shapes reputation, and defines your name.

In the long run, your ethical presence becomes your professional brand. People remember who asked questions when no one else would, who chose clarity over convenience, and who didn't join the quiet chorus of "everyone does it this way."

Quiet Tests of Integrity

Not every test of your values will be loud; some will be subtle. A phrase in a file, a suggestion in a meeting, and a moment when you feel the difference between what's easy and what's right.

In those moments, ethics becomes more than a personal value—it becomes a professional skill. Additionally, leadership, at its highest level, is ethical before it is anything else.

🔍 End-of-Chapter Reflection

Use these questions to reflect on how you handle ethical pressure and how you can grow into a leader known for integrity.

1. **When have I felt ethical tension in this role—and how did I respond in that moment?**

2. **Are there any areas where I've allowed silence or convenience to override my better judgment?**

3. **What does ethical leadership look like for me—and what will I do when it's tested?**

Part IV

Leading Through Communication

At a certain point in your adjusting career, communication shifts. It's no longer just about checking boxes or executing your role—it becomes something deeper. It becomes the way you influence, the way you lead, the way you shape the energy of a room, the direction of a decision, or the confidence of someone still finding their footing.

Leadership, particularly in claims work, involves less about position and more about presence. Regardless of whether you hold a title, your voice carries weight. It can set the tone for a team. It can reframe a tense conversation. It can provide steadiness in a room filled with noise. More often than not, it becomes the reason people look to you—not just for answers, but for clarity.

This section focuses on that shift. It's about moving from technical communication to transformational communication. From merely handling your workload to helping others grow in theirs. You'll explore how to adapt your style across generational differences, lead effectively in digital spaces where tone is often misinterpreted, support newer adjusters through modeling and mentorship, and develop a professional voice that others trust— even under pressure.

In today's ever-changing world, leadership is no longer defined by hierarchy; it's defined by how you show up. Great communication doesn't just help you get things done—it helps others rise with you.

Chapter 17

Communicating Across Generations

Modern claims work brings together professionals from different generations—each with distinct values, communication preferences, and professional rhythms. One adjuster may remember paper files and handwritten scopes, while another may have entered the field remotely, being fluent in digital platforms yet still finding their footing with tone and feedback.

"Every generation brings something valuable. Communication is how we bridge the difference—not reinforce the gap."

Even the definition of professionalism can shift depending on whom you're working with.

And yet, the file doesn't care how old you are. The policy doesn't ask for your birthday. The work demands collaboration, clarity, and connection—regardless of generation.

CURIOSITY OVER JUDGMENT

Communicating across generational lines is less about mastering clever techniques and more about cultivating curiosity, respect, and self-awareness. When we slow down long enough to understand what shapes someone's worldview—how they handle conflict, how they deliver feedback, or how they approach deadlines—we begin to build bridges instead of barriers.

For many adjusters, generational tension doesn't arise from malice—it stems from misalignment. A younger colleague may perceive directness as coldness. A more experienced team member might see frequent check-ins as micromanagement. These aren't character flaws; they're perceptual gaps. When we acknowledge them with empathy and adapt with intention, we create the conditions for genuine trust.

Every Generation Adds Value

The truth is that every generation brings something valuable to the table. Some offer deep institutional knowledge, while others bring fresh agility and systems thinking. What binds it all together is communication—calibrated, thoughtful, and flexible enough to transcend assumptions.

It's easy to slip into stereotypes, to dismiss a colleague's "old-school" habits or scoff at someone's "new-age" expectations. However, leadership in this space requires more; it asks us to choose understanding over judgment and to learn how to communicate in ways that make room for others, not just reinforce our own comfort zones.

Lead With Presence, Not Assumption

This doesn't mean abandoning your identity or overextending your emotional bandwidth. It means leading with presence, not assumption. It means paying attention to how someone receives guidance—not just delivering it on autopilot. It means showing patience when a process feels unfamiliar. And most importantly, it means challenging the myth that one generation has it all figured out.

From Effectiveness to Influence

When you communicate this way—whether to leadership, across to peers, or down to new hires—you move beyond effectiveness. You step into influence.

And that's the real turning point of this second edition. Communicating across generations is not just about navigating differences—it's about preparing to lead. It's about becoming the kind of communicator whose presence earns trust across roles, ages, and backgrounds. The type who doesn't just get the job done—but elevates everyone in the process.

🔍 End-of-Chapter Reflection

Consider how generational differences show up in your daily interactions—and how you can grow as a communicator who builds trust across perspectives.

1. *Where have I misunderstood or misjudged someone's communication style because it didn't match my own?*

2. *How can I lead with more presence and curiosity when working with people from different generations?*

3. *What would it mean for me to become a bridge—someone who makes space for difference while modeling consistency and clarity?*

Chapter 18

Virtual Adjusting & Remote Communication Mastery

The Shift from Physical to Virtual Presence

There was a time when most adjusting happened face to face—on rooftops, in driveways, or while walking through homes still carrying the weight of recent damage. Now, more and more of these interactions occur through screens, phone lines, apps, and digital documentation. Although virtual adjusting has created new efficiencies,

"Your writing becomes your presence when your voice can't be heard."

it has also introduced new risks—chief among them: miscommunication.

Remote environments strip away non-verbal cues that help people feel seen. They diminish the warmth and rhythm of natural conversation. What was once conveyed through a head nod, a firm handshake, or a quiet moment of empathy must now be communicated through typed words, scripted greetings, and calls with cameras off. In that gap, connection can be lost.

Leading Remotely Without Losing Humanity

But remote work doesn't have to imply distant leadership. In fact, some of the strongest communicators in this industry have learned how to make their presence felt even when their voice is the only thing someone hears.

That presence begins with intention. When you can't rely on visual cues or shared physical space, you must slow down and consider how each message might land. You start to notice the difference between a rushed email and one that anticipates confusion. You begin to think more critically about how tone is conveyed over the phone or how silence might be interpreted during a video call.

Clarity Becomes Non-Negotiable

You also start to take greater responsibility for clarity. Without the cushion of small talk or body language, ambiguity has less room to hide. You're either clear or confusing. And for policyholders navigating loss, or teammates managing stress, that distinction matters.

Mastering remote communication isn't about becoming robotic; it's about cultivating discipline. It involves making your words carry more weight without sounding cold and becoming the type of person whose professionalism remains intact even when the camera is off.

Pacing and Presence in a Blurred Workflow

It's also about pacing. When you're working virtually, it's easy for everything to blend together. One call slides into another. One email turns into a dozen. One deadline presses against the last. In that blur, it's easy to lose your tone, your patience, and your presence. That's when professionalism becomes performance—forced, thin, and barely sustainable.

Strong virtual adjusters know how to reset, build micro-moments of pause, reread before sending, and recenter between conversations so they don't carry tension from one file into the next. These aren't habits that show up in metrics, but they absolutely impact the claim experience.

Remote Doesn't Mean Emotionless

This work requires more than digital fluency; it demands emotional fluency. It involves the ability to stay grounded in what you offer, regardless of the platform. It also requires the capacity to make clients feel supported and teammates feel recognized—even when there's no physical handshake, no walk-through, and no office culture to rely on.

In the absence of proximity, leadership is reflected in tone. In a remote world, your tone becomes your brand.

THE VOICE THAT CUT THROUGH THE STATIC

It was a late afternoon during surge season, and my call queue was relentless. I picked up a call from a policyholder whose voice trembled with frustration. "I've sent five emails. No one's helping me," she said. I hadn't seen her file before, but I could hear the exhaustion behind her words.

I resisted the urge to defend the process or explain the backlog. Instead, I said, "You shouldn't have had to chase this down. I'm here now—and I'll stay with this until we have a path forward." Her tone softened immediately. We walked through the claim together, step by step, and by the end of the call, she thanked me—not for the outcome, but for being present.

That moment reminded me that virtual adjusting isn't just about tools and systems. It's about presence. It's about showing someone—through tone alone—that they are not invisible. And when technology strips away the non-verbal cues, your intention has to come through your voice.

🔍 End-of-Chapter Reflection

Use these questions to explore how you can bring greater presence, clarity, and leadership to your remote communication.

1. **How do I prepare myself to communicate clearly when I'm not in the same room with someone—and where might I be rushing or disconnecting?**

2. **What tone do I bring into emails, calls, or virtual meetings—and how might that tone be shaping trust, even when I don't realize it?**

3. **What would it look like for me to be known as someone who leads well—whether in person, on the phone, or from behind the screen?**

Chapter 19

Developing Your Communication Skills

Some people believe that communication is something you either have or you don't. However, the truth is that it's a skill, and like any skill, it can be practiced, refined, and strengthened over time.

"The strongest professionals are not the ones who have mastered communication— they are the ones still refining it."

Adjusters are not only asked to absorb information and make decisions— they're expected to communicate with clarity, write with authority, listen with patience, and navigate conflict with professionalism. That doesn't happen automatically; it occurs through intention, effort, and feedback, as well as through failure and repetition.

Progress, Not Perfection

The best communicators in this industry aren't perfect, but they are intentional. They learn to pause before sending messages. They ask better questions and stay curious when tension arises. They listen beyond words and choose their language not to impress, but to clarify. With every conversation—internal or external—they learn a little more about how their presence shapes outcomes.

What's most powerful about communication is its ability to evolve. You may start your career by rushing through difficult calls or writing notes that feel robotic. However, over time, with awareness and reflection, you learn. You become more grounded. Your voice becomes clearer. Your posture becomes more professional. Your questions become more precise.

And something shifts.

You stop merely getting through interactions—and start guiding them. You stop mirroring stress—and start calming it. You stop avoiding conflict—and start disarming it. That shift is subtle at first. But it's where leadership begins.

THE FIRST TIME I DIDN'T FLINCH

I'll never forget one of my earliest file reviews. I was on a virtual call with a senior manager, walking through my notes. Midway through, she stopped and said, "This denial—how did you deliver it?"

I froze. I hadn't considered tone. I hadn't rehearsed the phrasing. I simply told the policyholder it wasn't covered and moved on. Her next question hit harder: "Do you think they understood—or just heard you say no?"

That moment stayed with me. Not as a reprimand—but as a wake-up call. It was the first time I realized that communication isn't just about correctness; it's about care. I didn't flinch in the meeting, but I felt something change. From that day on, I read every claim note as if it could be read aloud. I practiced delivering hard news in a way that was firm but not cold. I still received denials—but I started getting thank-yous, too.

That's when I realized that the difference between being accurate and being effective is communication. Moreover, the difference between doing the job and earning trust lies in how you choose to speak.

The Rookie Who Helped Me Reset

During one hectic CAT deployment, I was on my seventh inspection of the day. I felt tired, was behind on notes, and was losing patience. I answered a team call with short, clipped responses—just trying to get through it.

Afterward, one of the newer adjusters messaged me privately. She said, "I know you're under pressure, and I've admired how you carry yourself. Just a heads-up—your tone today felt a little different. If it were me, I'd want someone to tell me."

Initially, I felt embarrassed. Then, I felt grateful. She wasn't correcting me—she was caring enough to be honest.

That message reset me. Not just for that day—but for my role as a communicator. It reminded me that the standard you set becomes the permission others take. And even when you're leading, you still have room to grow.

Communication as Influence

Because leadership isn't about authority—it's about impact. Your communication is one of the most immediate and lasting ways you influence people: your tone, your clarity, and your willingness to be honest, even when it's uncomfortable. These choices build trust or erode it.

The adjusters who rise in this field are not always the loudest or most experienced. They are often the ones who communicate thoughtfully, adapt without losing themselves, and model steadiness, even as everything around them shifts.

Sharpening the Skill That Elevates You

If you want to grow in this work—not just survive it but expand within it—let communication be the skill you keep sharpening. Not because someone told you to, but because you understand the power it gives you: to de-escalate a tense call, to clarify a claim decision, to restore trust when it's frayed, and to carry yourself in a way that earns respect even when the answer is no.

This second edition has focused on skills. However, it has also addressed identity. It aims to help you communicate not just to accomplish tasks—but to evolve into the type of professional you're proud to be.

The next level of that growth begins with ownership—an internal leadership that *Claim the Lead* is designed to support.

Because the better you communicate, the more confidently you lead—and the more clearly you begin to realize that you weren't just meant to handle claims. You were meant to lead something greater, starting with yourself.

🔍 End-of-Chapter Reflection

Use these questions to consider how communication has shaped your growth—and how you'll continue building the habits that define your professional presence.

1. *Which aspect of communication has grown the most for me—and what sparked that growth?*

2. *What habits or patterns am I still carrying that no longer serve my leadership or communication style?*

3. *How can I turn communication into a long-term investment in the professional—and leader—I want to become?*

Part V

The Adjuster's Inner Game

The most important skills in adjusting aren't always the ones others can see. Beneath the documentation, the scope notes, the phone calls, and estimates, there's a deeper layer of work happening—quiet, constant, and often overlooked.

This section is about that layer.

It's about the conversations you have with yourself in between the ones you have with clients. It's about how you recover after a long day, how you stand your ground under pressure, and how you protect your energy in a field that often demands more than it gives. It's about the habits you build, the stories you carry, and the invisible leadership you practice before anyone else sees it.

You've learned how to communicate under stress, how to collaborate across personalities, and how to navigate conflict with clarity. Now we turn inward—to the patterns that sustain or deplete you, and the choices that sharpen your edge or quietly wear you down.

In a role characterized by responsiveness, the real question becomes: how do you respond to yourself?

This final section isn't about performance; it's about presence. It's about building a relationship with your own capacity, protecting your clarity, and leading your inner world as skillfully as you lead others.

If you want to stay in this work, grow in it, and do it with integrity, you'll need more than just skill.

You'll need a system of care.

Chapter 20

Self-Care

This job will demand everything you give it. It will require your focus, your voice, your weekends, your lunch breaks, your patience, and your inbox. It can take your sleep if you allow it to. It will strip the softness from

"You can be excellent without being exhausted. You can lead without abandoning yourself."

your tone and the clarity from your mind.

It doesn't mean that—it's just the nature of the work.

Which is why the most quietly radical thing you can do as an adjuster is to care for yourself with intention. Not as an afterthought. Not as a reward for closing the last file. But as a non-negotiable part of your professional routine.

Burnout Doesn't Always Announce Itself

Here's the truth: burnt-out adjusters don't communicate well. They don't document thoroughly. They don't de-escalate with grace. They don't ask for help early.

Burnout doesn't always present as exhaustion. Sometimes it manifests as resentment. Sometimes it appears as withdrawal. At times, it shows up as cynicism disguised as sarcasm.

And when it strikes, everything else you've built—your tone, your reputation, your resilience—begins to erode.

That's where self-care becomes more than personal. It becomes professional.

THE DAY I ALMOST SNAPPED

It was a Monday afternoon during a storm response cycle. I was already behind, reliant on caffeine and adrenaline, jumping from one file to the next without taking a real breath. A policyholder called—angry, overwhelmed, and insistent that they'd been ignored.

I could feel my shoulders tense. My response came out tight— not rude, but clipped. I rushed to explain the process instead of truly hearing them. They grew increasingly upset.

After the call, I sat in silence, staring at my screen. I wasn't mad at them—I was mad at myself. I had nothing left in the tank, and it was apparent.

That night, I skipped dinner, answered emails from bed, and finally cried in the shower—not due to the claim, but because I had allowed the pressure to override my presence. That was the moment I stopped pretending I could outrun burnout.

The next day, I did something different: I blocked ten minutes between each call, took a full lunch break, informed my supervisor that I needed to slow my intake for 48 hours, and reminded myself—no claim is worth losing your center over.

That small reset saved more than just my schedule. It saved my voice, my empathy, and my decision-making. Now, when I sense myself slipping, I don't wait until it breaks. I guide myself back to calm before the damage occurs.

Capacity Is a Leadership Practice

Caring for yourself in this role involves managing your capacity. It means recognizing when your brain is too fried to write clearly, when your voice has gone flat, and when your empathy has run dry. It's about understanding that just because you can push through doesn't mean you should.

Real self-care isn't bubble baths and motivational quotes. It's about setting boundaries, creating systems, and taking the discipline to pause between calls to reset. It's about knowing when to stop multitasking because your judgment is slipping. It's about saying no when you need recovery—not because you're weak, but because you understand what sustainability requires.

The Adjusters Who Last, Lead Themselves

Some of the most respected adjusters in this industry aren't the ones who push the hardest—they're the ones who persevere the longest. Longevity in this field doesn't stem from brute force; it arises from emotional fluency, and from honoring your energy just as seriously as your deadlines.

It also comes from redefining what "strong" looks like.

Strength doesn't mean absorbing everyone's frustration and pretending you're fine. It means recognizing your limits and responding early. It means reaching out before the pressure leads to collapse. It means returning to yourself after a rough call—not with shame, but with gentleness.

You Lead Everything—Including Yourself

This work is noble. It's necessary. But it is not worth your health.

You can be excellent without being exhausted. You can be respected without being endlessly available. You can be calm without being passive, clear without being cold, and responsive without being reactive.

The key is learning to treat yourself as well as you treat others.

You lead the claim. You lead the conversation. You lead the tone.

You also lead your own wellbeing.

And that's a leadership decision worth making every single day.

🔍 End-of-Chapter Reflection

Use these questions to check in with yourself—not just as a professional, but as a person doing high-impact, emotionally demanding work.

1. **What signals does my body or mindset give me when I'm approaching burnout—and how often do I listen to them?**

2. **Where am I overextending in the name of productivity or professionalism—and what is that costing me long term?**

3. **What would it look like to lead myself with the same clarity, care, and boundaries I offer to everyone else?**

Chapter 21

Micro-Conversations That Matter

Most of your work will not occur in long meetings or formal presentations. It will happen in the moments in between. The 30-second explanation that calms someone down. The quick email that clarifies the next step. The firm but respectful tone you use to maintain a boundary. The voice you choose when someone asks, "Why wasn't this covered?"

"Leadership doesn't start with a title—it starts with the tone you bring to everyday moments."

These are the micro-conversations that shape everything.

They don't appear in performance reviews or call logs. Yet, they leave a mark—on your reputation, on the claimant's experience, and on the culture surrounding you. Over time, it's not your title or your resume that defines your professionalism. It's how you present yourself in those moments when no one is watching and no script exists.

Leadership Is Built in the Gaps

Every adjuster has these moments. You're pulled into a file you didn't start. A policyholder is already upset. A colleague has dropped the ball. You don't have all the answers—but you do have a choice: in how you respond, in how you speak, and in how you lead.

Leadership doesn't begin with a promotion. It begins in moments like these—when you realize your words can de-escalate conflict, offer reassurance, restore trust, or bring clarity to someone who's had a long day and a longer week. And it doesn't require big speeches or dramatic gestures; it just requires presence.

The Posture Behind Your Words

That's the invitation this chapter brings: to pay attention to the tone you use when you're tired, to notice how you explain something when the other person is clearly frustrated, and to reflect on the difference between saying, "That's not my responsibility," and, "Let me see what I can do to help redirect this."

The difference isn't in the words alone. It's in the posture behind them.

These small moments of communication are not small at all. They shape how people feel in your presence, whether they trust you, whether they listen to you, and whether they're willing to follow your lead, even when the outcome isn't what they hoped.

Every Word Builds or Breaks Trust

You can't control every reaction, but you can control how you contribute to the tone of the room—even if that room is a phone line, a file note, or a quick Slack message on a stressful day.

This chapter doesn't ask you to become perfect; it asks you to become aware. Once you realize how powerful your smallest interactions are, you stop wasting them. You stop using your voice carelessly and begin to become someone whose communication not only gets the job done but also leaves people better than you found them.

THE SLACK MESSAGE THAT SHIFTED EVERYTHING

It started with a file note from a field adjuster that made no sense. The documentation was thin, the estimate didn't match the photos, and I was already behind. Frustrated, I started to type a message in Slack: "Why was this even submitted like this?"

But I paused. I deleted the message and rewrote it: "Hey, I'm reviewing the file you submitted. I noticed a few things that look off. Can you help me understand what happened on site?"

Ten minutes later, I got a reply: "Thanks for reaching out. That day was chaos—I missed uploading a supplement. Let me fix it now."

That exchange could've gone another way. But choosing curiosity over criticism not only solved the issue faster—it strengthened trust. That's the power of micro-conversations. They happen fast, but their impact lingers.

You Are Already a Leader

In this work, you are already a leader—whether you've claimed the title or not.

The only question left is: *what kind of leader are you becoming?*

🔍 End-of-Chapter Reflection

Use these final questions to reflect on the tone, presence, and leadership you bring into even your smallest interactions.

1. **What is the tone I want to be remembered for—especially in quick or high-pressure moments?**

2. **Where have my smallest words or actions made the biggest difference in how someone felt about the claim?**

3. **What would it mean for me to lead more intentionally— not just in big decisions, but in micro-conversations that happen every day?**

Epilogue

From Communication to Leadership

If you've made it this far, it means you've done more than read a book.

You've paused to consider how you show up. You've questioned old habits. You've examined how your tone shapes trust, how your listening diffuses tension, and how your boundaries protect your energy. You've begun to recognize that communication isn't merely a skill—it's a form of self-leadership.

You've also proven something vital: that growth in this profession doesn't require a title. It requires awareness, integrity, and the willingness to lead from wherever you are—not because someone asked you to, but because you've decided that your presence should matter.

Because communication involves more than just what you say. It's how clearly you think, how deeply you care, and how skillfully you maintain clarity and compassion simultaneously.

This book wasn't just about technique—it was about becoming someone others can trust in uncertain moments. The person who doesn't just document facts, but guides decisions. The person who doesn't just speak, but listens. The one who doesn't just close claims, but builds relationships along the way.

But if this book has been about the how, then what comes next is about the who.

Who are you becoming when no one is watching?

Who are you when pressure builds and quick answers won't suffice? Who are you when the metrics are met—but something deeper still calls you higher?

If those questions stay with you, you're ready for what's next.

That's why Claim the Lead™ was created—to help adjusters step into a new kind of leadership. One built not on status, but on emotional presence, clarity, and performance under pressure. It serves as a guide for those ready to move from communication to culture-setting—from responding to leading.

And for those who feel the pull to go deeper still, the Mosaic Intelligence Method™ offers the next evolution. Some claims aren't just external—they live inside us. The hardest decisions aren't always in the file—they're in how we manage our own story, our emotional posture, and our place within a complex system.

The Mosaic Intelligence Method™ helps leaders integrate emotional integrity, cultural fluency, and identity awareness, especially during moments when leadership feels most personal. It doesn't ask you to be someone else; instead, it invites you to lead more fully as yourself.

Because the future of this work isn't just technical—it's human. The more whole you are, the more powerful your impact becomes.

Reflection Guide

For Adjusters Ready to Lead Themselves Well

This guide aims to help you pause, process, and internalize what this book offers—not just as a professional, but as a person engaged in emotionally complex, high-stakes work.

You can revisit these prompts individually, discuss them in a team setting, or use them to prepare for future leadership conversations.

There's no rush. No performance required. Just reflection.

---

1. Your Communication Identity

- What patterns have I noticed in how I speak, write, or listen under pressure?
- When do I feel most aligned in my communication—clear, calm, and confident?
- What's one phrase, tone, or habit I want to leave behind— and what do I want to replace it with?

---

2. Emotional Presence & Resilience

- When do I know I'm starting to shut down or overextend emotionally?
- How do I recover when a claim or conversation hits me harder than expected?
- What practice, boundary, or mindset could help me stay grounded without going numb?

---

3. Performance & Pace

- What does "high performance" look like for me now—and how is it different from burnout?
- How do I measure success in a day, outside of files closed or tasks completed?
- Where can I move with more focus—and where can I give myself more grace?

---

4. Team, Culture, and Contribution

- How am I shaping the tone of the teams I'm a part of—through energy, words, or silence?
- What kind of teammate or collaborator do I want to be remembered as?
- What would it look like to bring more consistency, support, or steadiness to the spaces I work in?

---

5. The Next Chapter of Your Growth

- Where do I feel a quiet pull toward something deeper—more leadership, more balance, more meaning?
- What conversations am I ready to have now that I wasn't ready for before reading this book?
- What am I willing to own—not just as an adjuster, but as a communicator and emerging leader?

This is the work before the promotion. Before the title. Before the training course.

This is the internal leadership that sustains your external impact.

When you're ready for more—*Claim the Lead* is here to guide your next step.

Final Note from the Author

This book began with a conversation—and it ends with an invitation.

You've spent these chapters not just learning communication strategies, but reflecting on how your presence shows up in every conversation, file note, denial explanation, and moment of silence. You've confronted the invisible weight of the work and examined your power to lead even when no one's watching.

That's the essence of this book: leadership without a title. Clarity without apology. Care without depletion.

In this industry, your voice matters. Not just for resolving claims—but for transforming the culture around how those claims are handled. If you take nothing else from this second edition, take this: communication is not just a task. It's a legacy. And every interaction you have is part of the reputation you're building.

So protect your energy. Speak with clarity. Lead with emotional steadiness. And never underestimate the power of your smallest decisions to shift someone's entire experience.

You are not just an adjuster. You are a communicator, a guide, a leader. And now more than ever, the industry needs voices like yours—strong, grounded, and human.

I'll see you in *Claim the Lead*.

Source References and Research Foundations

This book draws from a range of industry reports, leadership research, and communication frameworks relevant to the insurance adjusting profession. Below is a curated list of sources that informed key chapters, insights, and data points throughout the manuscript.

Industry Reports and Research Studies

McKinsey & Company. (2023). *The State of Workforce Resilience and Performance*.

Deloitte. (2022). *The Future of Claims: Navigating Complexity and Modernizing Operations*.

Harvard Business Review. (2021–2023). Articles on team dynamics, burnout, and emotional intelligence.

Insurance Information Institute. (2021). *Claims Cycle Time Trends and Adjuster Impact Reports*.

University of Michigan. (2020). *Organizational Trust and Turnover in High-Performance Cultures*.

National Association of Insurance Commissioners (NAIC). Ongoing regulatory updates and compliance resources.

Communication and Leadership Foundations

Daniel Goleman. *Emotional Intelligence: Why It Can Matter More Than IQ.*

Susan Scott. *Fierce Conversations: Achieving Success at Work & in Life One Conversation at a Time.*

Judith Glaser. *Conversational Intelligence: How Great Leaders Build Trust and Get Extraordinary Results.*

Crucial Conversations research (VitalSmarts/Crucial Learning)

Ethics, Self-Care, and Emotional Health

Mayo Clinic. (2023). *Burnout Symptoms and Prevention Strategies for Professionals.*

World Health Organization (WHO). Guidelines on stress management and emotional resilience.

American Psychological Association (APA). Research on emotional regulation and cognitive fatigue in workplace environments.

Insurance Journal. Articles on claims culture, adjuster retention, and ethical best practices.

Additional Field Sources

Composite insights from claims professionals, adjuster mentors, and leadership coaches

Case-based scenarios anonymized and adapted for educational purposes

Reflective practices aligned with CE course development standards

All references were selected to support real-world application in the fields of insurance, communication, leadership, and emotional wellness. Where applicable, field data was cited in narrative or footnote format within each chapter.

Bring Efficient Adjuster™ Training to Your Team

If this book resonated with you—or revealed gaps in communication, professionalism, or emotional resilience on your team—*Efficient Adjuster™* can help you go deeper.

We specialize in high-impact training for insurance professionals who want to raise the standard of communication, leadership, and performance in the claims environment. Whether you're a firm, carrier, or independent adjusting team, our programs are designed to meet the moment—with strategies that are real, relevant, and immediately applicable in the field.

Available Offerings:

CE-eligible workshops on communication, leadership, ethics, and wellness

Custom training sessions tailored to team dynamics, surge prep, or role transitions

Team coaching intensives for improving morale, conflict resolution, and cross-department collaboration

Licensing and onboarding support for adjusters navigating early-career growth

We work with adjusting firms, vendor partners, training departments, and solo professionals seeking to evolve—not just their skills, but their impact.

Ready to Train Differently?

Let's raise the standard—one conversation at a time.
Connect with us at: **EfficientAdjuster.net**
Or email: **training@efficientadjuster.net**

Continue Your Professional Development

If this book has provided you with valuable insights, take the next step in your journey with our specialized online courses designed to enhance your skills and confidence as an insurance adjuster.

Fast Emotional Reset Tools for Insurance Adjusters

A concise, 1-hour course offering practical techniques to manage stress and maintain composure during high-pressure situations.

Quick, actionable strategies for immediate application
Designed for busy professionals seeking rapid improvement
Enhances emotional regulation to improve client interactions

Enroll now: Fast Emotional Reset Tools for Insurance Adjusters

Communicate, Connect, and Lead™: Online Training Series

An in-depth, self-paced course expanding on the principles outlined in this book, aimed at developing advanced communication and leadership skills.

Comprehensive modules covering emotional intelligence, conflict resolution, and leadership
Interactive exercises to reinforce learning
Suitable for individual growth or team training programs

Explore the course: Communicate, Connect, and Lead™: Online Training Series

Why Choose These Courses?

Flexible learning: Access the material anytime, anywhere

Expert instruction: Learn from Dr. Karissa Thomas, a seasoned professional in the field

Practical application: Courses designed with real-world scenarios in mind

Visit Dr. Karissa Thomas's Udemy Profile: Dr. Karissa Thomas on Udemy

About the Author

Dr. Karissa Thomas is an award-winning author, educator, leadership strategist, and the founder of *Efficient Adjuster*™—a brand dedicated to elevating the communication, professionalism, and emotional intelligence of insurance adjusters nationwide.

With over a decade of cross-sector leadership experience in education, corporate training, and insurance claims, Dr. Thomas brings a rare blend of emotional fluency and operational insight to the world of adjusting. She has trained professionals across the U.S. and internationally, helping teams navigate high-volume environments, complex policy dynamics, and emotionally charged claims with greater clarity and confidence.

Her work spans catastrophe deployment, desk and field adjusting, leadership development, and continuing education instruction. She is also the creator of the *Claim the Lead*™ framework—an approach to internal leadership and performance resilience designed specifically for adjusters in high-pressure roles.

Dr. Thomas holds a doctorate in Educational Leadership and an Executive MBA. Her expertise in human-centered communication, cultural intelligence, and adult learning principles informs every book, course, and training she develops.

Through *Efficient Adjuster*™, she continues to equip claims professionals with the tools, mindset, and language to lead from any seat—because communication is more than a skill. It's a responsibility.

www.ingramcontent.com/pod-product-compliance
Lightning Source LLC
Chambersburg PA
CBHW031421120626
46545CB00006B/2215